HANDMADE MEMORIES

A Celebration of Quilts & Projects For Every Season

by **MISSOURI STAR QUILT CO.**

OPEN CAMERA, SCAN CODE, SEE BONUS DIGITAL EXTRAS
ON MISSOURIQUILTCO.COM

MISSOURI STAR
QUILT CO.

EXECUTIVE EDITOR
Natalie Earnheart

CREATIVE TEAM
Jenny Doan, Natalie Earnheart,
Misty Doan, Christine Ricks, Celeste
Rockwood-Jones, Mike Brunner,
Lauren Dorton, Jennifer Dowling,
Dustin Weant, Jessica Toye,
Kimberly Forman, Denise Lane

EDITOR & COPYWRITER
Nichole Spravzoff, Liz Gubernatis,
Lindsay Conner, Kevin Gubernatis,
Monique Jacobs

SEWIST TEAM
Jenny Doan, Natalie Earnheart,
Misty Doan, Courtenay Hughes,
Carol Henderson, Janice Richardson,
Cathleen Tripp

ADDITIONAL PHOTOGRAPHY
Derek Israelsen Studio,
Salt Lake City, UT

PRINTING COORDINATOR
Rob Stoebener

PRINTING SERVICES
Walsworth Print Group
803 South Missouri
Marceline, MO 64658

CONTACT US
Missouri Star Quilt Company
114 N Davis
Hamilton, MO 64644
888-571-1122
info@missouriquiltco.com

CONTENTS

138

146

158

166

188

202

INTRODUCTION

Holidays in my home are focused on food, family, and togetherness. We are makers at heart, whether it be homemade decorations, family-favorite cookies, or unique Halloween costumes. In my experience with my big, beautiful family, there is no such thing as a holiday that goes off without a hitch, but I wouldn't have it any other way.

NO MATTER WHAT WE MAKE, MESSES AND ALL,
IT'S REALLY ABOUT MAKING MEMORIES.

My children know that when we celebrate, it isn't about creating the perfect handmade gift or decorating a pristine Christmas tree. It's more about allowing ourselves to enjoy these important moments with the thought, What if? And I like to approach my quilting projects with the very same idea.

I've always said, "Any quilt can be a holiday quilt." I love recreating my favorite quilt patterns in an array of seasonal fabrics and we use them all year long. From Easter to New Year's Eve, and everything in between, each holiday has something to love. I always look forward to answering the door for neighborhood trick-or-treaters in their darling costumes. Thanksgiving is one of my favorite times of the entire year with family gathered around the table as we express gratitude and eat plenty of turkey. And to cap it all off, Christmas, with its anticipation and joy, fills my heart to the brim for the rest of the year.

Inside this book you'll find quite a few of my favorite seasonal projects for all of these wonderful holidays. Adding your own personal touch helps you create your own traditions and make memories. Don't forget: as you create your own beautiful quilts and handmade projects, allow them to be human. The point is to enjoy our time together, laughing through it all and embracing the joy and comfort of imperfection. There's no need to agonize about a stitch out of place. It's what makes you and everything you make truly unique. My hope is these holiday projects will inspire you and help you to celebrate all of the little, remarkable moments of life.

Jenny Doan
Missouri Star Quilt Co.

HOW TO CREATE A QUILT

Ready to make your own holiday-themed quilts and projects? Making a quilt is a rewarding process that starts with selecting your fabrics and picking the pattern that will make them sing "fa-la-la-la-la!" The projects in this book will take you from winter holidays and patriotic occasions to Halloween, Thanksgiving, and Valentine's Day. They are designed to suit a variety of skill levels, including new quilters and seasoned pros. By following along with the patterns in this book, you can create a variety of quilts and projects like wall hangings, table runners, bed-size quilts, a quilted stocking, patchwork tree skirt, and darling bags and zipper pouches.

Before you dive into making your first quilt, we want to share some of our tips and tricks for success. There is so much to learn from each step in the process, from measuring and cutting to quilting and binding. First-time quilters may want to come back to this section a few times for pointers as they stitch up their creations. We can't wait to see your finished projects! You can share them with us at #msqcshowandtell on social media.

Cutting Fabric

Are you ready to learn our must-have tools for cutting up quilting fabric?

☐ We recommend that quilters invest in and use a good rotary cutter (a 45mm size should do the trick) and a few extra blades to swap in when your current one gets dull. And don't forget to close that blade when you're done cutting—it's sharp!

☐ Next, you'll want to pick up an acrylic ruler, and it's a good idea to get a 6" x 24" size for cutting yardage, though a smaller size like 5" x 15" and 2.5" x 8" will work for slicing up precuts.

☐ Finally, you'll want a self-healing cutting mat. A large 36" x 24" mat will be useful for a variety of projects. But if you want to invest in a smaller size mat, that's perfectly fine to get you started.

To cut fabric with a rotary cutter, first place your cutting mat desk or table. You'll likely be standing here for a few minutes, so choose a comfortable height. Try not to sit while cutting, because you'll need that extra pressure and accuracy that comes from slicing fabric from directly overhead.

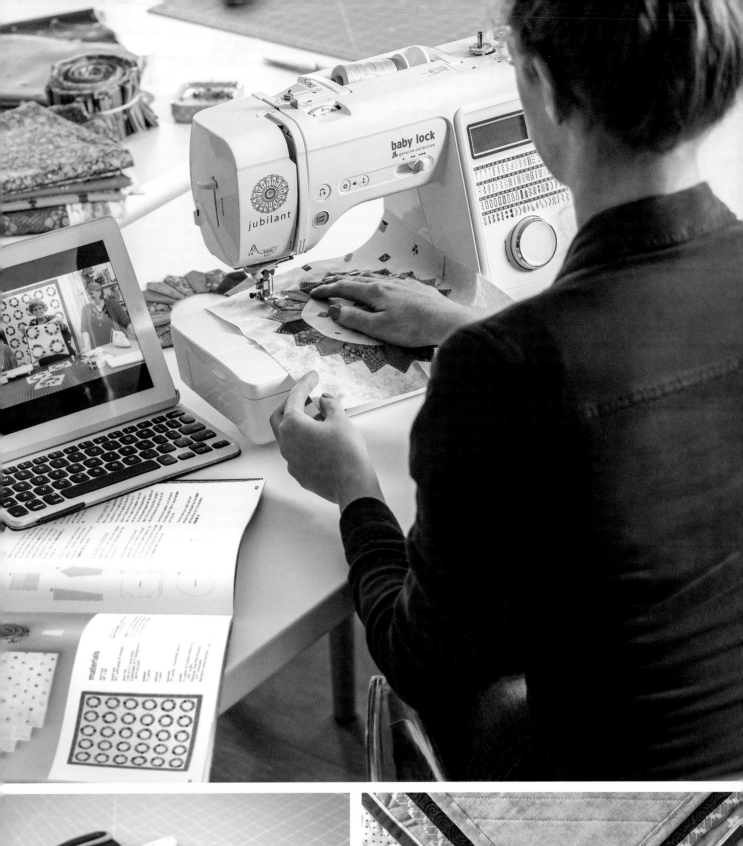

Take a look at the grid lines on your cutting mat and ruler. They will help you line up your fabric as you cut to get nice, straight lines. Safety first! Always hold the rotary cutter close to your body and cut in the opposite direction away from where you're standing. Use steady pressure and hold the ruler firmly with your non-dominant hand while cutting, keeping your fingers out of the way of the blade.

Want to make sure your cutting mat lasts a long time? To keep it from warping and getting bent out of shape, never iron fabric on it. Also, keep it away from warm places like heater vents and windows. Changing your blade often can also help extend the life of your mat.

Sewing

After the fabrics are cut, it's time to head to the sewing machine. Have you changed your needle lately? We recommend putting in a fresh 80/12 size universal quilting needle before starting a new project, or after about 8 hours of sewing. This will help you avoid skipped stitches and other inconsistencies. Also make sure you're using quality thread—grandma's vintage spools are pretty to look at, but they tend to break easily. A new 50 weight cotton thread will give you the best results when putting blocks together.

We'll be using ¼" seam for all the holiday projects throughout this book. Some sewing machines come with a ¼" foot to help you keep a consistent seam allowance. If you don't have one of these handy feet, a piece of tape or a seam guide can help you stay on track. **Tip**: Try not to worry too much about getting the perfect ¼" seam. If you use a consistent seam allowance the whole time you're sewing blocks, everything will line up just fine! Some projects in this book, like the *Winter Wall Hanging* on page 74, will call for appliqué, another trick to add to your quilting toolbelt. See *Tips & Tricks for Holiday Appliqué* on page 114 for a rundown on our favorite appliqué tools and methods.

Pressing, Trimming, & Squaring

The first step in getting your quilt blocks ready to join together is to press the seams. We recommend pressing seams toward the darker side when possible, so they aren't visible through lighter fabrics.

After the blocks are pressed, it's time to trim the edges. This is called squaring up a block. Square-shaped rulers are available in different sizes to help with this task, and they can be especially helpful for half-square triangles, as seen in the *Inside Out*

Heart on page 94 and the *Missouri Star Quilt* on page 20. **Tip:** If you don't have a square ruler, you can line up diagonal seams on your block with a 45° mark on your long ruler before trimming off that extra little bit of fabric.

Squaring up your blocks will help them sit nice and even when joined into rows. As you sew blocks together into rows, we recommend nesting the seams together. To do this, press one row of seams to the right and the next row of seams to the left. To join the rows, pin or clip them together at the seams. They should sew together snugly, creating less bulk.

After the last row is pieced together, you've got a quilt top! Press the quilt top, using some spray starch if you want to make it extra flat. Then trim and square up the entire top with a rotary cutter and the largest ruler you can find.

Backing

After your quilt top is pressed and trimmed, it's time to prepare your fabric backing. Measure the length and width of your quilt top, adding an extra 8 inches to both the length and width of your quilt if it's going to be machine quilted. You can piece together 42″ wide yardage to get the size you need, or use 108″ wide backing fabric for larger projects.

To piece the backing, first trim off all selvages and use a ½″ seam allowance to join the sections. Then sew the pieces together along the long edge. We like to press this seam allowance open, rather than to one side, to reduce the bulk. For small quilts (under 60″ wide), we place this backing seam horizontally on the quilt, but we use vertical seams for larger quilts. If you're using a print with a directional fabric, feel free to throw these rules out the window and position the fabric in

the way that makes sense with the front of your quilt.

Batting, Thread, & Quilting

Even though you won't see the batting in your finished quilt, you'll be able to feel its coziness and warmth. We recommend that beginners choose a cotton batting, which has a great feel and is easy to work with. Another good option is an 80/20 cotton-polyester blend batting, which has a nice drape. Both will complement your quilting design and will stand up well to many washes.

When choosing your quilting thread, we recommend that new quilters try to blend their thread color with the background of the quilt top. White, off-white, or gray thread can blend well with many fabrics. If your backing fabric is dark, you can use a darker thread in the bobbin and feed a lighter color thread through the machine. There are no rules when it comes to thread color, so feel free to be as bold as you'd like!

Basting is the process where you temporarily attach the three layers of the quilt—top, batting, and backing—together. Smooth out the layers and baste them together with basting spray (great for small projects) or safety pins (placed every few inches) before quilting. This ensures that the layers do not shift during machine quilting. And if you plan to send your quilt to a longarmer, you can skip this step altogether!

There are countless quilting designs you can choose, from free-motion machine stippling to straight-line quilting. Beginners may want to stitch in the ditch (sew directly on the major seams) to hide the thread or disregard the seams all together and choose an allover pattern like swirls or wavy lines. This can actually help hide errors in piecing.

Binding

After you've quilted your project and trimmed off the excess batting and backing, it's time to finish your quilt with binding—the frame to your finish! Binding comes readymade or you can create your own from yardage. We often like to make binding from 2½" jelly roll strips, because it's already cut and ready to sew. You can choose a fabric that's featured in the quilt top or a coordinating color for this step. We've listed yardage needed for binding for all of the holiday projects in this book.

Want to make your own binding? We recommend cutting fabric straight across the width of the fabric (through the selvages) or you make bias binding if you cut the 2½" strips on a 45 degree angle. You'll get to practice this for quilts with curved quilt edges like the *Christmas Tree Skirt* (pg. 40).

JOINING STRIPS – PLUS SIGN METHOD

To join binding strips together, lay one strip across the other with the right sides together, like a plus sign. Stitch from the top inside to the bottom outside corners crossing the intersections of fabric as you sew. Trim the seam to ¼" and press the center seam open to reduce bulk. Join as many strips together as you need to equal the perimeter of the quilt (the sum of all the edges) plus about 15" to 20" inches more to finish. The last step is to press the long strip in half widthwise to hide those seams, and you're ready to start binding your quilt!

MACHINE BINDING

There are many ways to bind a quilt, but we prefer to machine stitch it to the front of our quilt, then use an invisible slip stitch to hand sew it to the back. A ¼" seam allowance does the trick, as does leaving a 10" binding tail at the beginning and the end. Rather than starting the binding in a corner, we recommend starting off in the middle of one long edge.

MITERED CORNERS

Stop sewing about ¼" from the corner and take a backstitch. Remove the quilt from under the presser foot and clip your threads. Flip the binding up at a 90° angle to the edge just sewn, making a tiny triangle. The tail of the binding should point straight up. Then, fold the binding back down from the top edge, right next to the side that will be sewn next, aligning the raw edges. Sew from the top fold down on the next side, doing a little backstitch right at the beginning. This is how you can make perfect mitered corners every time.

CLOSING THE BINDING

When your needle is 12" away from the starting point, stop sewing! Remember those 10" binding tails we left at both ends? Lay them overtop each other and press a crease at their meeting point. Fold back the extra, measuring just 2½" inches of overlap. Trim off the rest of the binding strip and set it aside.

Use the plus sign method to match the edges and pin in place. Use a pencil or washable pen to mark your sewing line and stitch a straight line from the top inside corner to the bottom outside corner. After you press the seam open and fold the entire section of binding in half, it should rest neatly against the edge of your quilt. Stitch the binding down to the front side of your quilt, flip the edge over to the back side, and tack it in place with an invisible stitch or machine stitch.

USING PRECUTS

Here at Missouri Star Quilt Company, we're all about making quilting and sewing easier and more accessible than ever before. Precuts are the best thing since sliced bread! Precut fabrics are packages of fabric that are cut to size in advance. There's no need to cut fabrics for hours; they help you get right to the good part without all the fuss. Almost every single Missouri Star pattern is made to be used with precut fabrics, so all you need to know is how many precuts to choose of each size and you're good to go!

All these holiday quilts and projects are handpicked especially for precuts, along with a few tips and tricks to make sewing them together fast and fun. When you begin quilting with precut fabrics, it really couldn't be any easier. Keep on reading and learn how to make the most of each type of featured precut.

2½" PRECUT
Jelly Roll

2½"

This is how we roll! Jelly rolls or 2½" strips are one of the most popular precuts out there for a reason. They look so cute all rolled up and they are incredibly useful. It's almost a shame to open them up for a project, but it's totally worth it. If you've ever spent a good amount of time trying to cut perfect strips, you know how valuable these rolls are! From log cabin quilts to sashing and binding, 2½" strips get the job done. You can even slice them up into mini charms and use them to snowball corners and add cornerstones. There are just so many uses for these simple strips!

5" PRECUT
Charm Pack

5"

Prepare to be charmed! Charm packs are so cute and so easy to use. We like to keep them on hand for quick projects. Gather up a whole bunch of them and before you know it, they're quickly used right up without a single regret. These wonderful stacks of 5" squares can be used as-is for easy patchwork quilts or you cut them up into neat little quilt blocks that couldn't be simpler to create.

10" PRECUT
Layer Cake

10"

Layer cakes sound so delicious, don't they? These lovely stacks of fabric help big, beautiful quilts come together in a snap! Whenever we get our hands on one, they don't last long. We can't help but cut into them and get right to the good part—sewing! These fantastic 10" squares are perfect for quilters who are just starting out because of their versatility. You can do so much with a simple square. For example, you can make a quick set of eight half-square triangles with just two 10" squares. It's absolutely magical.

15

Any Quilt CAN BE A Holiday Quilt

Holidays are a big deal in my house. From big family get-togethers and memories made around the dinner table to decorations around every turn, there's no doubt that we love to celebrate!

But, let's face it, not every holiday is going to get you revved up to make a quilt. For instance, I know some people don't celebrate Valentine's Day, shrugging it off as a holiday sponsored by Hallmark to sell more cards. Others don't appreciate the spookiness of Halloween or the myth of a big guy who comes down your chimney. And that's okay! Because I want to let you in on a big secret. . . .

YOU CAN MAKE ANY QUILT A HOLIDAY QUILT
—AND ANY HOLIDAY, AT THAT!

What? That's right! With some savvy design choices, you can take any quilt and adapt it to fit any occasion. So pick any pattern that calls to you. Can you envision it in holiday fabrics? What if you actually pulled some fabrics together and sewed up a sample block, or used quilt design software to mock up the pattern in a new colorway? As you scroll Instagram or pick up a quilting book or magazine, keep your eyes peeled for possible chameleons—the quilts that are just begging to have their colors changed.

Now obviously, changing a Thanksgiving wall hanging with turkey blocks to a Halloween quilt with cat blocks is going to take a few extra steps. But throughout this book, we want to inspire you to see holiday quilts in a new light. You can adapt any quilt to celebrate any occasion or season you choose! Sub out Christmas fat quarters for patriotic prints, and now your quilt is ready for the Fourth of July picnic. Swap hearts for ghosts, Easter hues for rich fall tones, and pick up novelty prints that match the vibe you're going for.

We're going to teach you multiple ways to style quilts for the holidays all year long. Each holiday quilt in this book also includes an alternative holiday rendition. We want to empower you to make bold design choices and embrace the fun of quilting! It's not just about following a pattern, but putting your own creative spin on it. Here are some design tips to keep in mind when designing quilts for the holidays.

Picking Fabric: Color, Scale & Style

We also have a few basic ways to shop for fabric, and that is to consider their color, print style, and print scale. Learning to think in these terms will help you curate fabric for your next holiday quilt and many more to come.

COLOR

I often like to think in color in terms of the four seasons—winter, spring, summer, and fall. Although you may live somewhere that doesn't have distinct seasons, many people associate each season with certain colors. For instance:

> **WINTER:** White, blue, grey, silver, or colors that convey snow and ice

> **SPRING:** Green, bright, or pastel shades that mimic new growth

> **SUMMER:** Yellow, orange, watermelon, or happy colors

> **FALL:** Brown, dark orange, deep red, or muted shades of falling leaves

Of course, holidays can often have their own traditional colors regardless of their season. I instantly think of Mardi Gras when I see the colors purple, green, and gold together in a quilt. What colors do you associate with each holiday? Try to think about how you use or have seen others use holiday color stories in quilting. It's fine to break the rules once you know them, like subbing in hot pink with green for a fun twist on Christmas colors. But we bet you've never made a Christmas tree skirt in red, white, and blue!

When considering colors, it's important to note that not all blues (or reds or greens) are created equally. Remember to choose fabrics with a bit of contrast—lights, mediums, and darks—if you want your blocks to pop. Ignoring color value (i.e. including all fabrics of the same intensity) can make your quilt look muddy or flat.

PRINT SCALE

Big prints, small prints, medium prints—oh my! Particularly with novelty fabrics, the scale or size of a print absolutely lends itself to some holiday projects more than others. Even if the colors are perfect for fall, you probably won't sew a Thanksgiving table runner from T-Rex fabric. You'd be more likely to choose pumpkins and leaves. Of course, tiny dinosaurs that read as a tone-on-tone fabric could actually work. It's fun to play around with scale, but try not to use only prints of the same scale. You need a place for your eye to rest, after all. When the fabrics are too busy, all your eye sees is a big mess. As you'll find in these patterns, you can use small, medium, and large-scale prints in your holiday quilts as long as you choose them thoughtfully.

As a general rule of thumb, bigger prints tend to work well in small quilts, as they are less likely to overwhelm your eyes. If your print is very busy, give it some room to breathe with a solid sashing or border. Smaller prints can often read as solids from far away. On small quilts and table toppers, the scale of a print will be much more "in your face," so feel free to audition your fabrics by laying them out, taking some photos, and walking away. Come back later with fresh eyes and see what you think of them all together.

PRINT STYLE

Classic, cozy, elegant, modern—your fabric choice probably has a lot to say about your personal style. So what's your cup of tea? Understanding your personal style and why you gravitate toward certain prints or colors can help you make better choices in the future and stash up on more fabrics you'll actually use. Our quiz, *What's Your Seasonal Style* on page 36 can help you explore your distinct tastes for fabric.

Have you ever known a quilter who has a closet of gray T-shirts but really lets loose when it comes to their quilts? Quilting is a safe space to explore your love for bold florals and animal prints without having to wear them. What prints and styles do you like? Is your ideal Valentine's print filled with candy hearts or a floral that works well into spring? At Halloween, do you prefer fabrics that trend creepy or cute? Does your Christmas décor lean more traditional, sophisticated, kitschy, or modern? These are some good questions to ask yourself to get a feel for your fabric style.

No matter what fabrics you choose, go with your gut, and have fun with the process! Pretty soon you'll be an expert at curating holiday fabric bundles and making any quilt you see a holiday quilt for any holiday you like!

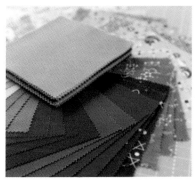

MISSOURI STAR QUILT

Which is our favorite block of all time, you ask? Well, it's none other than our namesake, the

Missouri Star Block, of course! It's big, bold, and colorful—perfect in every way. Make one

for yourself. It just might become your favorite too!

MATERIALS

QUILT SIZE 74" x 97" | **BLOCK SIZE** 23½" unfinished, 23" finished

QUILT TOP

1 package of 10" print squares

4 yards of background fabric

BORDER

1 yard

BINDING

¾ yard

BACKING

6 yards - vertical seam(s) or 3 yards of 108" wide

STEP 1: sort & cut

Select (12) 10" print squares for the center squares and trim each to 9½".

Set aside (24) 10" print squares for the quarter-square triangles and 6 squares for another project.

From the background fabric, cut:

- (3) 9½" strips across the width of the fabric—subcut into (12) 9½" squares.

- (8) 7" strips across the width of the fabric—subcut into (48) 7" squares.

- (8) 6¼" strips across the width of the fabric—subcut into (48) 6¼" squares.

STEP 2: make the center squares

Layer a 9½" background square atop a 9½" print square, right sides facing. Sew around the perimeter. Cut the sewn squares twice diagonally. Open and press each unit, then square to 6¼". Each set of sewn squares will yield 4 half-square triangles. **2A 2B**

Arrange the 4 half-square triangles in 2 rows of 2 as shown. Sew the units together in rows and press in opposite directions. Nest the seams and sew the rows together to complete 1 center square to 12", if necessary. **Make 12.** **2C 2D**

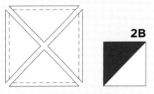

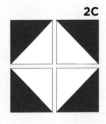

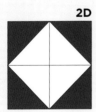

STEP 3: make quarter-square triangles

Lay a 10″ print square atop a differing 10″ print square, right sides together. Cut both squares in half vertically and horizontally to create 4 pairs of 5″ squares.

Keep the 5″ print squares right sides facing and sew down 2 opposite sides of each pair. **3A**

Cut the sewn squares in half diagonally—2 from the top left to the bottom right; 2 from the bottom left to the top right. Open and press to get mirror images. *They must be opposite angles.* Each set of sewn squares will yield 8 quarter-square triangles. **3B 3C**

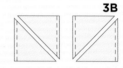

Cut (4) 7″ background squares in half diagonally. Fold each triangle in half and fingerpress to mark the center of the long edge **3D**

Lay a background triangle, right sides together, atop the quarter-square triangle, and match the fold of the background triangle to the seam of the quarter-square triangle. Sew them together along their long edges. Press, then square to 6¼.″ **3E**

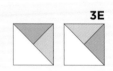

Repeat with (11) 10″ print squares and (44) 7″ background squares to **make 12** sets of 8 matching print quarter-square triangles. Each set will have 4 units with the prints set in reverse order of the other 4 units.

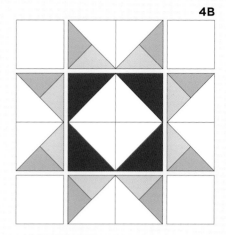

4B

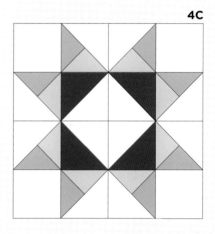

4C

STEP 4: block construction

Select 1 set of quarter-square triangles. Sew 2 units side-by-side as shown. **Make 4**. **4A**

Arrange 1 center square, (4) 6¼" background squares, and the 4 units you just made in 3 rows of 3 as shown. **4B**

Sew the units together in rows and press in opposite directions. Nest the seams and sew the rows together. Press. **Make 12**. **4C**

Block Size: 23½" unfinished, 23" finished

STEP 5: arrange & sew

Refer to the diagram **5A** to lay out your units in **4 rows of 3**. Sew the blocks together in rows. Press the seams in opposite directions. Nest the seams and sew the rows together. Press.

STEP 6: border

Cut (9) 3" strips across the width of the border fabric. Sew the strips together to make 1 long strip. Trim the borders from this strip. Measure, cut, and attach the borders to the quilt top. The strip lengths are approximately 92½" for the sides and 74½" for the top and bottom.

STEP 7: quilt & bind

Refer to the finishing sections of *How to Create a Quilt* on pages 12-14 to quilt, square and trim, then add binding to finish your quilt.

5A

1 To make the quarter-square triangles needed for the legs, sew the 5″ pairs together with 2 parallel seams on opposite sides.

2 Lay the 4 pairs on the mat with the same fabric facing up. Cut all in half diagonally: 2 from the bottom right to the upper left; 2 from the bottom left to the upper right.

3 Lay the quarter-square triangle and creased background triangle right sides together and match the seam with the crease.

4 Sew them together along their long edges.

1 PATRIOTIC

PALETTE

A Patriotic explosion of Red, White and Blue, we alternated the star points on this quilt to add a little sparkle. Using three colors but alternating placement makes the same pattern sing a whole new anthem.

2 HALLOWEEN

PALETTE

Made again in Halloween prints, we used a spooky-cute line with a gray background to let the Halloween holiday colors pop!

DALA HORSE RUNNER

The Dala horse is a traditional carved, painted wooden statue of a horse. In modern times it has become a symbol of Sweden in general. These sweet Dala horses carved from fabric adorn our table runner—and any meaningful symbol can make this table runner perfect for your favorite holiday!

MATERIALS

PROJECT SIZE
16½" X 39"

PROJECT TOP	OUTER BORDER	OTHER
(6) 10" squares	½ yard	Freezer paper
¼ yard coordinating fabric - includes sashing and inner border		Glue stick (optional)
	BINDING	
	½ yard	
(1) 12" red felt square or (1) 12" red square & (1) 12" fusible interfacing	**BACKING**	
	½ yard	

STEP 1: cut

Cut each of the 10″ print squares in half
to yield (12) 5″ x 10″ print rectangles. Set 6
different rectangles aside for another project.

From the coordinating fabric, cut (4) 1½″
strips across the width of the fabric. Subcut 2
strips into a **total of (7)** 1½″ x 10″ rectangles.
Set 2 rectangles and the remaining 2 strips
aside for the inner border.

STEP 2: arrange & sew

Lay the print rectangles in 1 row as shown.
Place a 1½″ x 10″ sashing strip between each
rectangle. Sew the row together. Press. **2A**

STEP 3: inner border

Refer to diagram **5B** on page 32 for the
inner and outer borders. Use the 1½″ x 10″
coordinating fabric rectangles set aside
earlier for the side borders. Trim the top and
bottom borders from the 1½″ coordinating
strips set aside previously. Measure, cut,
and attach the inner borders to the project
top. The strip lengths are 34½″ for the top
and bottom.

STEP 4: outer border

Cut (3) 3″ strips across the width of the
fabric. Sew the strips together to make 1
long strip. Measure, cut, and attach the inner
borders to the project top. The strip lengths
are approximately 12″ for the sides and 39½″
for the top and bottom.

STEP 5: appliqué shapes

Trace the horse and heart shapes provided
on page 212 onto the non-waxy side of
freezer paper. Trace a second horse, facing
right, to the non-waxy side of the freezer
paper. Rough cut around the tracings, then
iron to the felt, waxy side down. **5A**

2A

5A

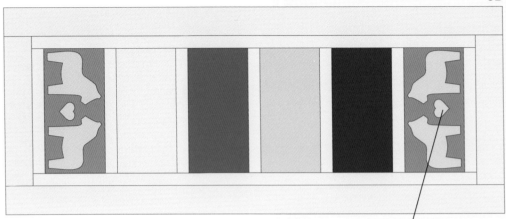

5B

5C

Cut along the traced lines. Remove the freezer paper by lightly heating with the iron. Reposition to use again. Make a **total of 2** left-facing horses, a **total of 2** right-facing horses, and a **total of 2** hearts.

If you are using fabric instead of felt, following the manufacturer's instructions to fuse the interfacing to the back of the fabric first, then use the freezer paper method to make the horses and hearts.

Iron, pin, or glue the appliqué shapes to the first and last blocks of the runner as shown. **5B**

Appliqué the horses and hearts into place using either a zig-zag or blanket stitch. **5C**

STEP 6: quilt & bind

Refer to the finishing sections of *How to Create a Quilt* on pages 12-14 to quilt, square and trim, then add binding to finish your project.

1 Cut the 10" squares of your selected fabrics in half once. Use 1 of the 5" x 10" rectangles of each fabric.

2 Sew sashing strips between the rectangles.

3 The sequence: rectangle, sashing, rectangle, sashing.

4 Appliqué the shapes to the first and last rectangles of the runner using a zigzag or blanket stitch.

///////////////////////////////// **MIX IT UP!** /////////////////////////////////

1 VALENTINES

PALETTE

Sweet and simple, this sophisticated version is black, white, and red—for the perfect Valentines look that carries over all the way to Mother's Day.

2 EASTER

PALETTE

This Easter runner uses soft pastels to pull together a truly happy and hoppy runner that's at home on any table during the Season of Renewal. Find our bunny template on page 212.

3 HALLOWEEN

PALETTE

The Spooky Cat runner is the perfect project for laying out treats for your tricksters on Halloween. We used a bright pink and orange to set off both ends in this version, coupled with candy prints on white, these fabrics sparkle! Our Spooky Cat template can be found on page 212.

4 HARVEST

PALETTE

An awesome autumnal version has all the harvest feels. In these cozy warm tones, you can almost taste the apple pie and pumpkin spice!

WHAT'S YOUR SEASONAL STYLE?

Is your Easter table always pastel or are you bright and bold and jewel-toned? Do you lean gothic Halloween dripping with a hint of ruby red or are you more a creepy/cute character fan? You probably know what you like when you see it—and you may see it differently depending on the holiday! Are you a playful patriotic but an elegant Christmas? Take our quiz below to see what your seasonal style inspires! Choose your holiday and answer each question—collect your answers for results that may surprise you!

1 Pull a Color Palette

A Keep it simple with a two-color palette

B An unexpected color splash, anything out of the ordinary

C Spectrum of color—the entire rainbow!

D Bright colors on a black background

E A monochromatic color palette with a pop of color

2 Turn on Your Favorite Tunes

A Country

B Jazz

C Pop

D Rock

E Classical

3 Grab a Sewing Snack

A Toast with jam

B Hummus and carrots

C Peanut butter and apple slices

D Cheese and crackers

E A few pieces of chocolate

4 And a Drink, While You're At It

A Hot cocoa

B Lemon water with cucumber

C A fruity drink

D Chocolate milk

E Chamomile tea

5 Your Sewing Space is:

A Cozy and cluttered

B Bright and beautiful

C Filled with fabric

D Piled with unfinished projects

E Organized and efficient

6 Your Favorite Sewing Notion is:

A Your grandmother's thimble

B Your favorite hera marker

C Your matching set of cutting tools

D Your trusty seam ripper

E Your powerful iron

7 When is your favorite time to sew?

A Right when you wake up

B Whenever you feel inspired

C On the weekends

D Anytime at all!

E At night

8 How do you like to start a new project?

A Open up a quilting book and choose a traditional pattern

B Find a vintage block and change it up

C Go for a walk outside and see what colors inspire you

D Dream up your own design and sketch it out

E Carefully select a quilt kit and stick with it from start to finish

9 When creating a quilt, what is your favorite part?

A Hand quilting

B Creating your own unique design

C Pulling a mix of beautiful fabrics from your stash

D Fussy cutting cute prints

E Stitching on the binding

10 Pick the word that best describes your quilting personality:

A Steadfast

B Innovative

C Cheerful

D Spontaneous

E Refined

RESULTS!

MOSTLY A
YOUR SEASONAL STYLE IS CLASSIC

When you celebrate, it's all about tradition. Your grandmother's quilts grace the beds and your style has a timeless quality. For you, each holiday is focused on savoring the moment and what better way to enjoy the changing seasons than spending quality time with your loved ones right at home.

MOSTLY B
YOUR SEASONAL STYLE IS MODERN

Taking cues from classic quilts and going beyond is your forte. You appreciate traditions, but you also enjoy trying out new seasonal trends and keeping your style fresh and new. When holidays happen at your home, it's anything but the expected and it's always inspiring.

MOSTLY C
YOUR SEASONAL STYLE IS COLORFUL

There's hardly a speck of white space on your walls and there's absolutely nothing wrong with that! Each holiday is colorful and bright at your home and it's sure to be stylish. Go ahead and celebrate with a spectrum of color no matter the season!

MOSTLY D
YOUR SEASONAL STYLE IS PLAYFUL

Each holiday is warm and bright at your house. The parties go late and the music is always playing. Having fun is always in style and you make sure there's plenty of it to go around. When neighbors come knocking, you're quick to invite them in. Can we be invited too?

MOSTLY E
YOUR SEASONAL STYLE IS ELEGANT

Understated and elegant, your home is peaceful and serene. Your celebrations are simple with tasteful details that are sure to be appreciated. You prefer to enjoy each holiday without all the extra fuss and focus on creating a festive atmosphere with subtle details that truly shine.

1 WINTER

The holiday season is a time of comfort and warmth. It's about savoring time together and celebrating all the reasons we feel joy. These festive projects have been chosen to help you create a cozy, welcoming atmosphere in your home. Handmade touches remind us of days gone by and create new memories. From patchwork stockings hanging by the fire to homemade ornaments for the tree that even the kids can create, take time to dress up your home and enjoy a holiday to remember.

CHRISTMAS TREE SKIRT

Finally, a Christmas tree skirt that you can make up as quickly as Santa can wink his twinkling

eyes. Pick up 2 packages of 5″ print squares and a little border fabric and you'll be all set to sew!

MATERIALS

PROJECT SIZE
45″ x 45″

PROJECT TOP
2 packages of 5″ print squares

BORDER
½ yard

BINDING
1 yard - includes ties

BACKING
3 yards - vertical seam(s)

OPTIONAL SUPPLIES
Freezer paper

Fabric pen

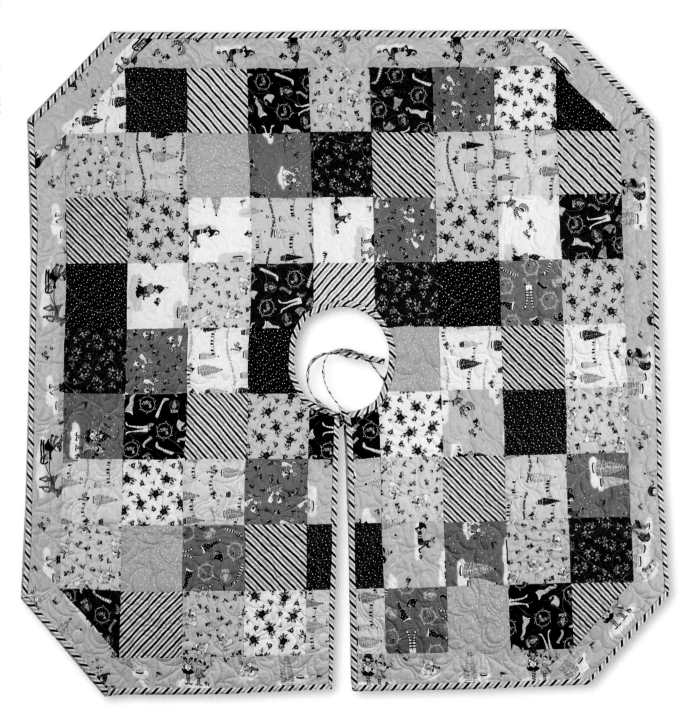

STEP 1: lay out the top

Lay out the squares in **9 rows of 9**. When you are happy with your arrangement, sew the squares together to form rows. Press the rows in opposite directions. Nest the seams and sew the rows together. Press. **1A**

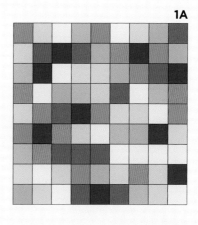

STEP 2: border

Cut (6) 2¾″ strips across the width of the fabric. Sew the strips together to make 1 long strip. Trim the borders from this strip. Measure, cut, and attach the borders to the project top. The lengths are approximately 41″ for the sides, 45½″ for the top and bottom, and (4) 15″ strips for the corners.

Sew the side borders in place then add the top and bottom borders. **2A**

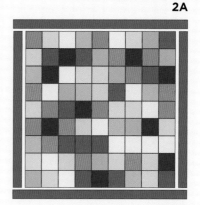

In 1 corner, use a removable fabric pen to mark a diagonal line that crosses the corner square on a 45° angle as shown. Trim the corner ¼″ away from the marked line. Repeat for all 4 corners. **2B**

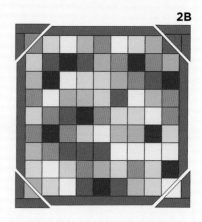

Sew a border strip to the corner of the project. Trim the strip evenly with the edge of the project on both sides. Repeat for the remaining corners. **2C**

STEP 3: finishing

Layer the project with batting and backing and quilt.

Find the center of the tree skirt by folding it in half lengthwise, then vertically. Mark the center with a pin or a fabric pen.

Trace a 4¼″ circle using the template provided on page 214 onto a piece of freezer paper. Cut out the freezer paper

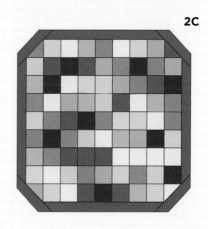

1 Add the border strips to the outer edges of the quilt.

2 Trim each corner at a 45-degree angle.

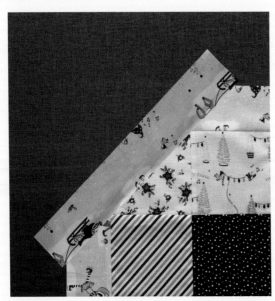

3 Add a short border strip to each corner.

4 Trim the ends of the corner border strips evenly with the edges of the quilt.

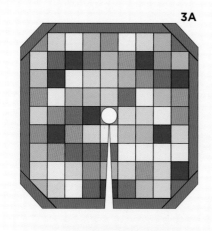

3A

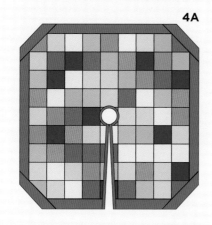

4A

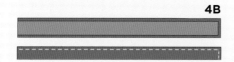

4B

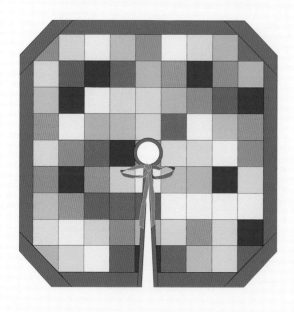

circle and press the shiny side of the paper to the center of the tree skirt. On 1 side of the skirt, draw a line from the circle to the outer edge. Cut along the line and around the circle. **3A**

STEP 4: make bias binding & ties

Because of the center circle, you will need to make bias binding. From the binding fabric, cut a 30″ strip across the width. Subcut a 30″ square. Set the remaining fabric aside for the moment.

Fold the square once on the diagonal. Press a crease in place along the diagonal fold, being careful not to stretch the fabric. Place a ruler perpendicular to the fold and cut at least (10) 2½″ bias strips. You'll need enough strips to total at least 275″ once the strips have been sewn together. Refer to Binding on page 14 of *How to Create a Quilt* and use the Plus Sign method to join the strips.

After the strips have been joined, gently press the strip in half with wrong sides together. Match and sew the binding to the unfinished edges of the tree skirt, including the split and the circle. Turn the folded binding edge to the back, then whipstitch in place to complete your project. See Binding (pg. 14) for binding instructions. **4A**

From the binding fabric you set aside earlier, cut (1) 1¼″ strip across the width. Subcut (2) 1¼″ x 12″ rectangles. Press each rectangle under ¼″ along the long sides and on 1 end. Fold the rectangles in half with wrong sides facing. Topstitch close to the pressed edges to finish the tie. **4B**

Sew a tie to both sides of the circle to complete your tree skirt, tucking the raw edges of the tie under the tree skirt.

1 CHRISTMAS 1

PALETTE

We chose this modern palette with light cheerful blue and pink added to classic red and green and finished with a striped binding—sugarplums and candy canes are dancing under this tree!

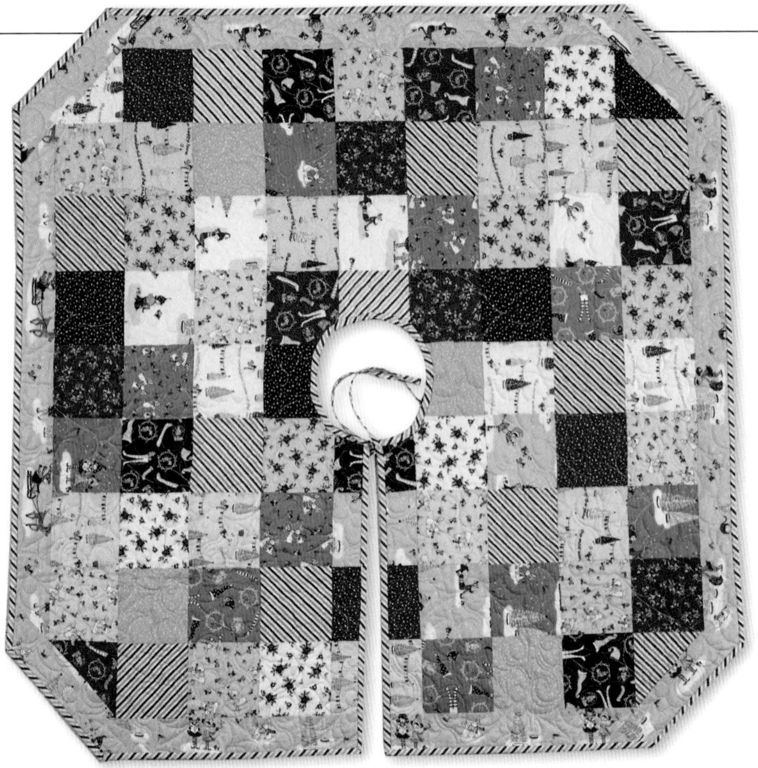

2 CHRISTMAS 2

PALETTE

Reds, Greens, Grays and Florals make this patchwork tree skirt classic and contemporary. The red binding is a perfect accent color to dress up your tree!

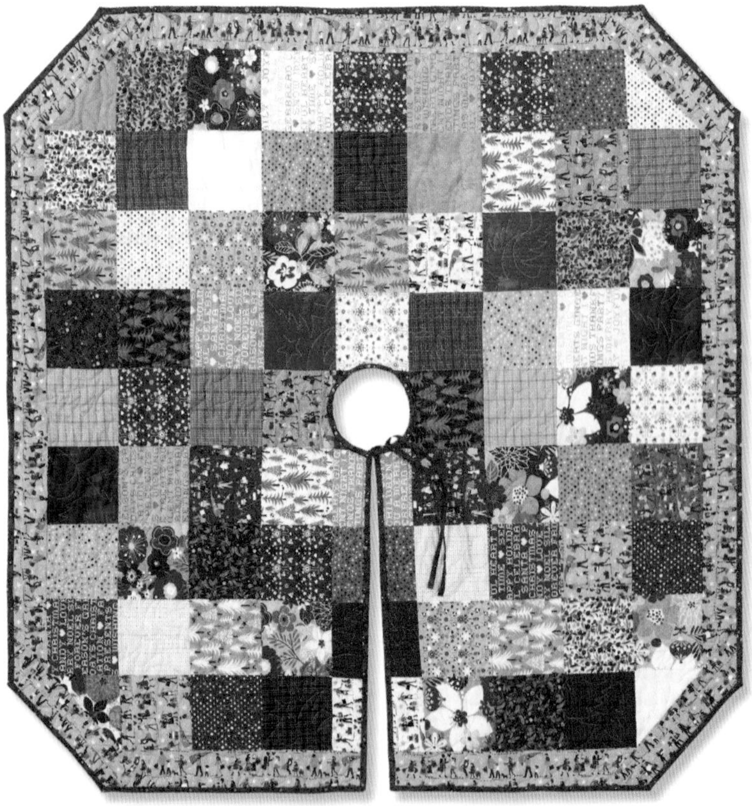

PLAID CHRISTMAS, I GAVE YOU MY HEART...

A photo of me with my two oldest daughters, Natalie and Sarah, in front of the Christmas tree.
And look at the pattern on that couch!

PATCHWORK STOCKING

Simple squares turn into the sweetest patchwork stocking! We've made this with easy

cuffs and straight-line quilting. Whatever your seasonal style, a patchwork stocking is

sew fun to make!

MATERIALS

PROJECT SIZE
12" x 17"

PROJECT SUPPLIES

1 package of 5" print squares

¾ yard of print fabric for each stocking*

For more variation, ¼ yard of coordinating print can be used for each cuff.

Missouri Star Quilter's Best Blend Crib Batting

STEP 1: make 4-patches

For each stocking, pair (5) 5″ light print squares with (5) 5″ dark print squares. Lay 1 pair of squares right sides together. Sew along 2 opposite sides. Cut the pair in half parallel to the seams. Open and press towards the darker fabric. Repeat with the remaining pairs of squares. Set the remaining 5″ squares aside for another project. **1A**

Sew the units together end-to-end in 1 long strip, alternating light and dark prints, and nesting seams. Press. **1B**

Cut (1) 2½″ increment from the end of the pieced strip. **1C**

Fold the remaining half of the first segment, right sides facing, over the next segment in the pieced strip. Cut along the edge of the folded piece as shown. Continue folding and cutting the segments into 4-patch blocks. Press. You will have a **total of (9)** 4-patch blocks and a **total of (2)** 2-patch blocks. **1D 1E**

STEP 2: arrange & sew

Arrange (8) 4-patch blocks in **4 rows of 2** as shown. When you are happy with the layout, sew the blocks together to form rows. Press the rows in opposite directions. Nest the seams and sew the rows together. Press. **2A**

Sew the remaining 4-patch block to a 2-patch block to create the toe section. Set the remaining 2-patch block aside for another project. **2B**

Sew the toe section to the bottom of the right side of the stocking unit as shown. **2C**

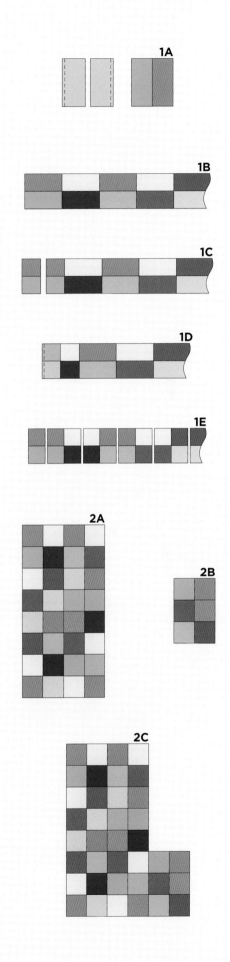

STEP 3: quilt & construct

From the print fabric, cut (1) 18″ strip across the width of the fabric. Subcut (2) 18″ x 14″ rectangles for the lining and backing. Set the remainder of the strip and fabric aside for the moment.

Cut (1) 14″ x 18″ rectangle from the batting.

Layer the stocking on top of the batting and lining. Quilt as desired. Trim around the entire stocking. Round off the toe and heel using a plate, jar, or glass to help mark the curve. **3A**

Lay the quilted stocking front atop the 18″ x 14″ backing rectangle, right sides facing, and pin in place. Sew the pieces together along the edge of the stocking using a ¼″ seam allowance. Start at the top, stitch down around the heel and toe, then back up—leaving the top open. Backstitch at the beginning and end. Trim off the excess backing. Clip curves and turn right side out.

STEP 4: make a loop

From the print strip you set aside earlier, trim (1) 1½″ strip across the width of the fabric. Cut (1) 1½″ x 5″ print rectangle.

Fold the strip in half lengthwise with wrong sides together. Press. Open the strap and press both raw edges in toward the center crease. **4A**

Refold the strip and stitch the strap closed ⅛″ from the edge. **4B**

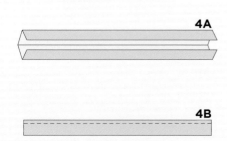

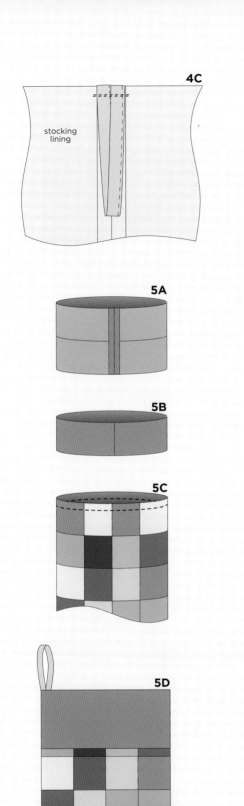

Fold the loop in half. Position it inside the stocking on the back seam. Its raw edges should line up with the stocking's raw edges, as shown. Double stitch across the loop at about ⅜″ from the top edge. **4C**

STEP 5: make the cuff

Trim the remainder of the print strip you set aside earlier, to 8″ x 16½″.

Fold the print rectangle in half lengthwise wrong sides together and press. Open. With right sides together, sew the short sides together—creating a tube. **5A**

Turn the tube right side out. Fold the cuff in half again along the fold, matching the raw edges. **5B**

Place the cuff inside the stocking, lining the raw edges of the cuff and stocking together. Sew a ½″ seam around the top. **5C**

Turn the cuff to the outside and pull up the loop. Press. **5D**

Your stocking is ready for Christmas!

1 Sew all the blocks together in one long strip. Fold over the first block on the far left at the seam. Cut at 2½". Voilà! (1) 4-patch.

2 Sew the toe section to the stocking—on either side, it's your call!

3 Layer the stocking on backing and batting.

4 Quilt as desired.

//////////////////////////////////// **MIX IT UP!** ////////////////////////////////////

1 CHRISTMAS 1

PALETTE

A playful print, classic reds, and a fun splash of greens with both black and white accents, you could make cuffs of several coordinating colors for everyone in your home.

2 CHRISTMAS 2

PALETTE

Modern reds and greens with snowflake cuffs, these patchwork stockings add a handmade look to the hearth of home and cabin, both.

SIMPLE SQUARES ON POINT

Get straight to the point with a quilt that's simply stunning without the stress. Instead of piecing

squares on the diagonal, skip all the fuss and do a bit of clever cutting to create the on point

design after you piece!

MATERIALS

QUILT SIZE 96″ x 96″ | **BLOCK SIZE** 10″ unfinished, 9½″ finished

QUILT TOP

2 packages of 10″ print squares

1 roll of 2½″ solid strips*

INNER BORDER

¾ yard

OUTER BORDER

1¾ yards

BINDING

¾ yard

BACKING

8¾ yards - vertical seam(s) or 3 yards of 108″ wide

*2¾ yards of solid fabric cut into (36) 2½″ strips can be substituted.

STEP 1: sort & cut

Select 36 light prints and 36 dark prints from your packages of 10″ print squares and set the rest aside for another project. You will have a **total of 72** print squares. Keep the light and dark prints stacked separately.

Set (4) 2½″ solid strips aside for another project. From the remaining 36 solid strips, cut (4) 2½″ x 10½″ rectangles from each strip for a **total of 144** rectangles.

STEP 2: block construction

Place a 2½″ x 10½″ solid rectangle on top of a 10″ light print square with right sides facing. The rectangle needs to be angled approximately 2″ in from the edge of the square at the top and at least ½″ in from the bottom edge. Sew the rectangle in place using a ¼″ seam allowance. Press the strip over the seam allowance toward the outer edge of the square. **2A 2B**

Repeat for 1 adjacent side of the square. Notice how the wider portions of the rectangles are on the opposite corner of the square. **2C 2D**

Turn the square over so the reverse side is facing up. Using the square as a guide, trim off the excess fabric showing beyond the edges. Flip the square back over so the right side is facing up. **2E 2F**

Add a rectangle to the 2 remaining sides of the square using the same process as before. Notice how the wider portions of the rectangles cross over each other. **2G**

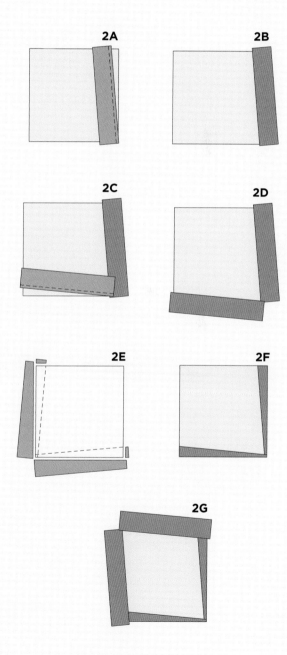

2A 2B 2C 2D 2E 2F 2G

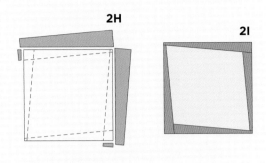

Again, turn the reverse side of the square up. Trim as before to complete a Diamond Paver block. **Make 36** Diamond Paver blocks using the solid rectangles and light print squares. **2H 2I**

Block Size: 10″ unfinished, 9½″ finished

STEP 3: arrange & sew

Arrange the blocks and dark print squares into **6 rows of 6**. Notice the orientation of the Diamond Paver blocks. Each odd row will begin with a Diamond Paver block and alternate with a dark print square. Each even row will begin with a dark print square and alternate with a Diamond Paver block. Press the rows in opposite directions. Nest the seams and sew the rows together to make 1 large square. Press the seams toward the bottom. **Make 2** large squares. **3A**

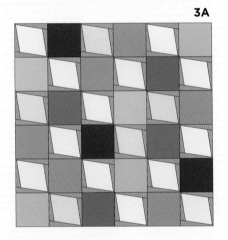

Turn 1 of the large squares 90° as shown. Sew the 2 large squares together to make 1 large rectangle. Press the sea toward the top. **3B**

STEP 4: mark & cut

Align a straight edge with the upper right corner and the lower left corner of the bottom of the sixth row of squares. Make sure the straight edge is intersecting the corner of each block and mark the diagonal. Cut on the diagonal, being careful not to stretch or tug on the edges.

Without moving the project, realign the straight edge with the top of the first square on the left side of row 7 and the bottom of the last square on the right in row 12. Again, make sure the straight edge is intersecting the corner of each block. Carefully mark, then cut on the diagonal.

Number each section and draw an arrow beside the number so you can keep track of which direction each section is oriented. Refer to the diagram for labeling the sections. **4A**

STEP 5: rearrange & sew

Pick up Section 3 and place it to the right of Section 1. Make sure the arrows still point in the same direction as before. Pick up Section 2 and place it under Section 3. **5A**

Sew Section 3 and Section 2 together. Press the seam allowances toward Section 2.

Make sure all block seam allowances are aligned and then sew Section 1 to the left. Press the seam toward Section 1.

STEP 6: inner border

Refer to diagram **6A** on page 62 for the inner and outer borders.

Cut (9) 2½″ strips across the width of the inner border fabric. Sew the strips together to make 1 long strip. Trim the borders from this strip. Measure, cut, and attach the inner borders to the quilt top.

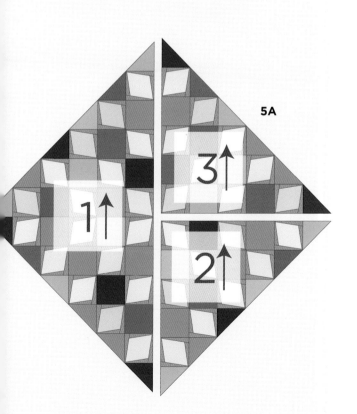

The lengths are approximately 81½″ for the sides and 85½″ for the top and bottom.

STEP 7: outer border

Cut (9) 6″ strips across the width of the outer border fabric. Sew the strips together to make 1 long strip. Trim the borders from this strip. Measure, cut, and attach the outer borders to the quilt top. The lengths are approximately 85½″ for the sides and 96½″ for the top and bottom.

STEP 8: quilt & bind

Refer to the finishing sections of *How to Create a Quilt* on pages 12-14 to quilt, square and trim, then add binding to finish your quilt.

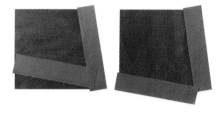

1 Place a 2¼" x 10¼" solid rectangle on top of a 10" light print square with right sides facing and angled approximately 2" in from the edge of the square at the top and at least ¼" in from the bottom edge. Sew the rectangle in place. Press the rectangle over the seam allowance.

2 Repeat for 1 adjacent side of the square.

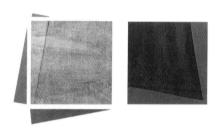

3 Turn the square over so the reverse side is facing up. Using the square as a guide, trim off the excess fabric showing beyond the edges. Flip the square back over so the right side is facing up.

4 Add a rectangle to the 2 remaining sides of the square using the same process as before. Notice how the wider portions of the rectangles cross over each other.

5 Again, turn the reverse side of the square up. Trim as before.

6 Make 36 Diamond Paver blocks using the solid rectangles and light print squares.

HANDMADE GIFTS SPARKLE ALL THE BRIGHTER

Ron found and re-worked these bikes so all the kids would have something to ride.
We stayed up all night making Hillary a doll house. We've always cherished handmade memories.

//////////////////////////////////// **MIX IT UP!** ////////////////////////////////////

1 | **PATRIOTIC**

PALETTE

For a little red, white, and vroom, we paired this motorcycle-themed novelty print collection with our denim blues accent fabric and made a patriotic quilt perfect for our 4th of July picnic.

HEXAGON ORNAMENT TABLE RUNNER

We love pretty red holiday word fabric, candy cane striped binding, and classic Rankin Bass

Christmas characters! Novelty print fabrics can be a blast from Christmas past! Santa, Rudolf,

the Snowman and all of your favorites are here, to make your holiday season bright! A few

simple steps turn your favorite fabrics into a trio of ornaments to decorate your table.

MATERIALS

PROJECT SIZE
18¼" x 36¼"

BLOCK SIZE
10" x 10¾" unfinished,
9½" x 10¼" finished

PROJECT TOP
(6) 10" print squares

¼ yard background
- includes inner borders

(1) 5" black square

OUTER BORDER
¼ yard

BINDING
¼ yard

BACKING
¼ yard

ADDITIONAL SUPPLIES
Missouri Star Large Half
Hexagon Template for
10" Squares

10" square fusible
interfacing

¼ yard tiny black rickrack

STEP 1: cut

Fold each of the (3) 10" print squares in half. Use the Large Half-Hexagon Template (pg. 213) to cut 2 half-hexagons from each folded square as shown for a **total of 6. 1A**

From the background fabric:

Cut (1) 4⅝" strip across the width of the fabric.

- Subcut into (6) 4⅝" x 6" rectangles.

- Fold each 4⅝" x 6" rectangle in half. Cut the set-in pieces by placing the narrow side of the template ½" in as shown. Cut around the template. **Make 12** pieces—6 mirrored pairs. **1B 1C**

Cut (3) 1½" strips across the width of the fabric. Set these aside for the inner border.

STEP 2: block construction

Attach a set-in piece to both sides of 2 matching half-hexagons. Align the set-in's narrow top to the wide bottom of the half-hexagon. Sew with right sides facing along the angled edge. **2A**

Press to the dark fabric. **2B**

Cut (3) 2½" strips from the remaining 10" squares. Fingerpress the center. Fold each half-hexagon in half and fingerpress the center of its long, bottom edge. Sew a strip between 2 half-hexagons of the same print as shown. Press. **2C**

Trim the block's sides ¼" beyond the outer point of the half-hexagons. **Make 3**. **2D**

Block size: 10" x 10¾" unfinished, 9½" x 10¼" finished

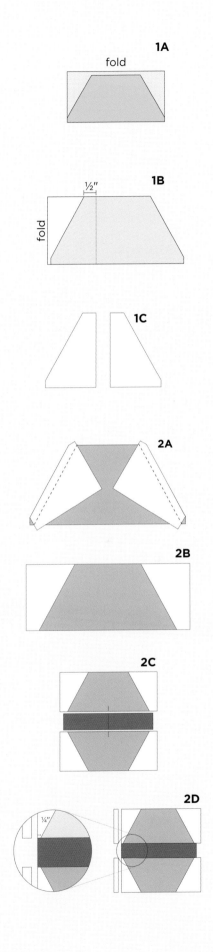

Sew the 3 blocks together into a row. Press. **2E**

STEP 3: inner border

Gather the (3) 1½" background strips you set aside earlier. Trim the 2 side borders from 1 strip and trim the top and bottom borders from the remaining 2 strips. Measure, cut, and attach the inner borders to the project top. The lengths are approximately 10¾" for the sides and 31" for the top and bottom. **3A**

STEP 4: outer border

Cut (3) 3½" strips across the width of the outer border fabric. Trim the 2 side borders from 1 strip and trim the top and bottom borders from the remaining 2 strips. Measure, cut, and attach the outer borders to the project top. The lengths are approximately 12¾" for the sides and 37" for the top and bottom. **3A**

STEP 5: ornament tops

Iron the fusible interfacing to the back of the 5" black square. Cut (3) 1½" x 2½" rectangles. Snip off the top corners at a 45° angle approximately ½". **4A**

Place ornament tops on table runner as shown. Sandwich a short rickrack piece approximately 4" long behind the ornament hanger top. Fuse in place on the runner. Appliqué the ornament top with a blanket or zigzag stitch to secure in place. Turn the rickrack into the shape of a hanger. Stitch down.

STEP 6: quilt & bind

Refer to the finishing sections of *How to Create a Quilt* on pages 12-14 to quilt, square and trim, then add binding to finish your project.

2E

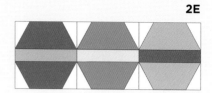

3A

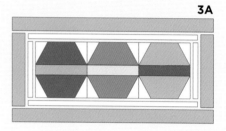

4A

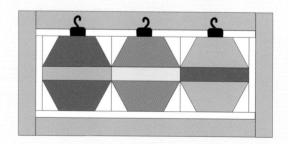

1   Fold (3) 10″ print squares using the 10″ hexagon shape to cut 2 half hexagons from each 10″ square.

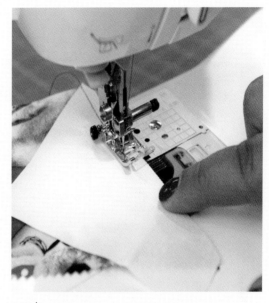

2   Attach set-in pieces to the slanted sides of each hexagon.

3   Use a 10″ strip to connect the top and bottom portions of the ornaments, wide edges facing each other. Center all 3 elements.

4   Trim the block to the 10″ center strip.

////////////////////////////////////// **MIX IT UP!** //////////////////////////////////////

1 **CHRISTMAS 2**

PALETTE

Shiny baubles in elegant flourishes—for this table runner,
we love how the dark ornament and stripe coordinate with
the metallic silver and bright red.

2 **THANKSGIVING**

PALETTE

This take on the table runner swaps the appliquéd ornament hanger
for a sturdy stem on this trio of batik pumpkins. A dark background
and fun border turn this into a perfect Thanksgiving project! Find our
pumpkin stem template on page 213.

HANDMADE STOCKINGS, SMILES, AND SIBLINGS

Left-to-right, our seven children with the stockings I made for them. Al, Sarah,
Natalie (holding Josh), Hillary, and Darrell (holding Jake).

WINTER
WALL HANGING

Deck the halls in style with this wall hanging quilt project! You're sure to get on the 'Nice'

list with this quick and easy project featuring festive presents, stars, trees, and gnomes. Put it

together with a bit of cuddle for 3D beards—such a fun detail!—and you'll have something to

hang by the chimney with care in time for the holidays.

MATERIALS

PROJECT SIZE

48" x 42"

PROJECT TOP

1 package of 10" print squares

1½ yards background fabric
- includes inner border

¼ yard cuddle fabric

OUTER BORDER

¾ yard

BINDING

½ yard

BACKING

3 yards - vertical seam(s)

OTHER

Missouri Star Large Simple Wedge Template for 10" Squares

Missouri Star Large Half Hexagon Template for 10" Squares

STEP 1: stars

Select (4) 10" print squares and cut (2) 2½" strips across the width. Subcut 5 matching 2½" squares from each pair of strips for a **total of (20)** 2½" print squares.

Cut (3) 2½" strips across the width of the background fabric. Subcut **total of (32) 2½"** background squares. From the remaining strip, cut (4) 2½" x 6½" rectangles and (1) 2½" x 8½" rectangle. Set the remaining fabric aside for now.

Place a 2½" print square on an angle (any angle) atop a 2½" background square with right sides together. Sew ¼" in from the angled edge of the print square. Trim ¼" away from the sewn seam. **1A**

Press the print piece over the seam allowance. Trim the edges evenly with the background square. Keep the trimmed scrap. **1B 1C**

Use the scrap from the first leg of the star to make another leg on the opposite side of the square. Make sure the second leg crosses over the first by at least ¼". Stitch, press, and trim as before. **1D 1E 1F**

Gather (4) 2½" background squares, 4 matching star leg units, and (1) 2½" matching print square. Arrange the pieces to form a 9-patch and sew together.

Sew (1) 2½" x 6½" background rectangle to 1 side of the unit to complete the Star Block. **Make 4** Star Blocks. **1G**

Block Size: 6½" x 8½" unfinished, 6" x 8" finished

1A

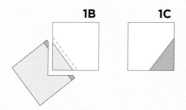

1B   1C

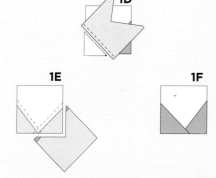

1D

1E   1F

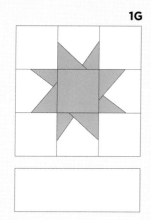

1G

Sew 4 Star Blocks together in a row as shown. Press. Sew (1) 2½" x 8½" background rectangle to the right side of the row. Press toward the background rectangle. Set aside until you are ready to assemble the quilt top. **1H**

Section Size: 26½" x 8½" unfinished, 26" x 8" finished

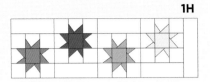

STEP 2: gnomes

Select (4) 10" print squares—2 for the gnome bodies and 2 for their hats.

Cut 2 wedges from (2) 10" print squares using the Large Simple Wedge Template found on pg. 215.

Cut 2 half-hexagons from each of (2) 10" print squares using the Large Half Hexagon Template pg. 213 for a **total of 4.**

Cut (1) 4¾" strip across the width of the background fabric. Subcut 4 half-hexagons from the strip using the template. Cut each half-hexagon in half for a **total of 8.**

Cut (1) 10" strip across the width of the background fabric. Subcut the strip into (2) 10" x 16" rectangles.

Fold the (2) 10" x 16" rectangles in half, aligning the 10" sides. Align the Simple Wedge Template as shown. **2A**

Cut along the right edge. Open the fabric, reposition the template, and continue cutting the right side of the wedge across the remainder of the fabric. **2B**

Repeat to cut a wedge from the second rectangle.

Sew the print wedge to the left portion of the background rectangle, matching the bottom edge. Press toward the print fabric. Sew the right background rectangle to the pieced unit to make

Fold of fabric

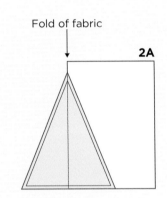

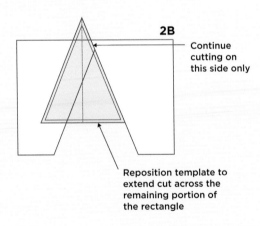

Continue cutting on this side only

Reposition template to extend cut across the remaining portion of the rectangle

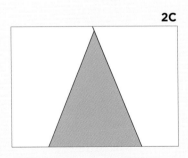

2D

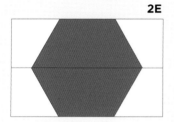

2E

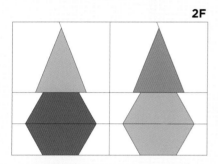

2F

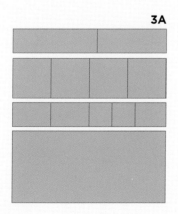

3A

the Gnome's hat. Press toward the background fabric. Trim this unit to 13½" x 9½". **2C**

Repeat to **make 2** Gnome Hat units.

Sew 2 halves of half-hexagons to the angled sides of each print half-hexagon. Press toward the background fabric. **Make 4** units. **2D**

Sew the matching, pieced half-hexagon units together to create the Gnome's Body. Press the seam in 1 direction. Trim the unit to 13½" x 8½" if necessary. Repeat to **make 2** Gnome Body units. **2E**

Sew 1 Gnome Hat unit to the top of 1 Gnome Body unit. Press toward the Gnome Body unit. Repeat to **make 2** Gnome Blocks.

Block Size: 13½" x 17½" unfinished, 13" x 17" finished

Sew 2 Gnome Blocks together and press to 1 side. Set aside until you are ready to assemble the quilt top. **2F**

Section Size: 26½" x 17½" unfinished, 26" x 17" finished

Note: The beards for the gnomes will be added after the wall hanging has been quilted.

Option: If you don't like the fluffiness of our cuddly beards, you could substitute a quilting cotton fabric and appliqué the beard onto your quilt top before or after quilting.

STEP 3: gifts

Select (4) 10" print squares. From each 10" square, cut:

- (1) 2¼" strip across the square. Subcut (4) 2¼" squares from each print.

- (2) 1¼" strips across the square.
  - Subcut (1) 1½" x 5½" rectangle, (2) 1¼" x 2¼" rectangles, and

(2) 1¼" squares from each print. **3A**
From the background fabric, cut:

- (1) 1¼" strip across the width of the fabric.
  - Subcut (4) 1¼" x 3" rectangles and (8) 1¼" x 1¼" rectangles.

- (2) 2¼" strips across the width of the fabric.
  - Subcut (1) 2¼" x 26¼" rectangle and (3) 2¼" x 6¼" rectangles for sashing.

Select 4 matching 2¼" print squares. Pair the squares with (1) 1¼" x 5¼" rectangle and (2) 1¼" x 2¼" rectangles of a contrasting print fabric.

Sew a 2¼" square to both sides of a 1¼" x 2¼" rectangle. **Make 2** units. Press towards the rectangle. Sew a unit to both sides of a 1¼" x 5¼" rectangle. Press toward the rectangle. **3B**

On the wrong side of each 1½" print square, draw a line once on the diagonal. **3C**

Place a marked 1½" print square on the left side of a 1½" x 3" background rectangle with right sides facing. Sew along the drawn line, trim the excess fabric away ¼" from the sewn seam. Open and press. Repeat for the right side of the rectangle. **3D 3E 3F**

Sew (1) 1½" x 1¾" rectangle of background fabric to the left and right sides of each these units. **3G**

Sew 1 Bow unit to the top of the Gift Box unit that has the same print fabric for the ribbon. Press toward the Gift Box unit. **Make 4** Gift Blocks. **3H**

Block Size: 5½" x 6½" unfinished, 5" x 6" finished

Sew the Gift Blocks together in a row separated by 2½" x 6½" sashing. Press toward the sashing. Sew the 2½" x 26½"

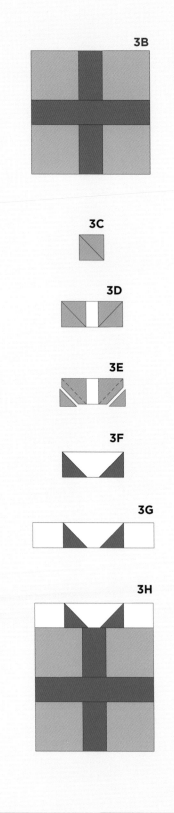

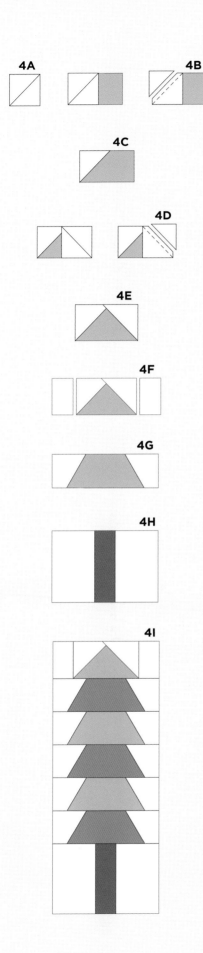

sashing strip to the top of the unit and press toward the sashing. Set aside until you are ready to assemble the quilt top. **3I**

Section Size: 26½" x 8½" unfinished, 26" x 8" finished

STEP 4: tree

Select 3-4 green 10" print squares to make the tree body and 1 brown 10" print square for the tree trunk. From each green square, cut (2) 5" x 10" rectangles. From 5 of these rectangles, cut 5 half-hexagons using the template (pg. 213). Trim 1 rectangle to 5" x 8¼".

Cut (1) 3" x 9¼" rectangle from the brown print square for the tree trunk.

Cut (2) 4¼" strips across the width of the background fabric—cut half-hexagons from the strip using the template. Each strip will yield 4 half-hexagons and 5 are needed. Cut each of the 5 half-hexagons in half for a **total of 10.**

Cut (1) 5¼" strip across the width of the background fabric. Subcut (2) 5¼" x 9¼" rectangles.

Trim the remaining strip to 5" wide. Subcut (2) 5" x 3" rectangles and (2) 5" squares.

Draw a diagonal line once on the reverse size of (2) 5" background squares. **4A**

Place a marked square on the left side of the 5" x 8½" green print rectangle, right sides facing. Sew on the line. Trim ¼" away from the seam and press toward the triangle. **4B 4C**

Repeat for the other side, as shown.**4D 4E**

Sew (1) 5" x 3" background rectangle to both sides of this unit. **4F**

Sew 2 halves of background fabric half-hexagons to the angled sides of each of the green print half-hexagon. Press toward the background fabric. **Make 5** half-hexagon units. **4G**

Sew the (2) 9½" x 5½" rectangles to both side of the 3" x 9½" print rectangle. Press toward the center rectangle to make the trunk unit. **4H**

Sew the flying geese unit, the 5 pieced half-hexagon units, and the trunk unit together in a column, in that order. Press toward the trunk. **4I**

Trim the block to 13½" x 33½" if necessary. Set aside until you are ready to assemble the quilt top.

Block Size: 13½" x 33½" unfinished, 13" x 33" finished

STEP 5: arrange & sew

Sew the Stars to the top of the Gnomes. Add the Gifts to the bottom. Sew the Tree Block to the right side. Refer to diagram **5A** below, if necessary.

STEP 6: inner border

Cut (2) 2½" strips across the width of the background fabric. Trim the strips for the inner border from these. **Note**: The inner border is only on the bottom and left side of the quilt.

Measure, cut, and attach the inner borders to the project top. The strip lengths are approximately 39¼" for the bottom and 35¼" for the left side. **5A**.

Attach the bottom inner border first and the left inner border second. **5A**.

STEP 7: outer border

Cut (5) 4" strips across the width of the border fabric. Sew the strips together to make 1 long strip. Trim the borders from this strip. Measure, cut, and attach the outer borders to the project top. The strip lengths are approximately 41½" for the top and bottom and 42½" for the side borders.

STEP 8: quilt & bind

Refer to the finishing sections of *How to Create a Quilt* on pages 12-14 to quilt, square and trim, then add binding to finish your quilt.

STEP 9: add the beards

Cut 2 beards from cuddle fabric following the templates on page 215. Attach the beards to the wall hanging as shown in diagram **5A**.

Use a vacuum along the edges of the beard after you cut it to remove any excess fluffiness.

TIPS & TRICKS

5A

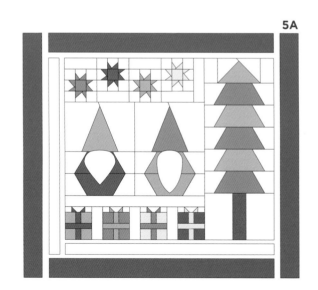

1 Fold a 10″ x 16″ background rectangle in half. Place the centerline of the Simple Wedge Template on top of the fold with the short side of the template even with the bottom of the fabric. Cut along the edge of the template to remove a wedge shape from the triangle.

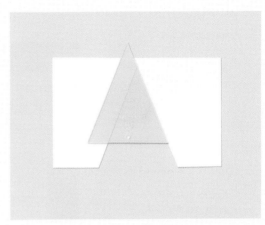

2 Unfold the fabric and lay the template on top matching the right edge of the ruler with the right edge of the wedge you just cut from the rectangle. Make sure the template extends past the top of the fabric and continue cutting along the right edge of the template to yield 2 separate pieces from the rectangle.

3 Sew a print wedge to the left portion of the background rectangle. Press toward the print wedge. Trim any excess background fabric even with the print wedge.

4 Sew the right portion of the background rectangle to the right edge of the print wedge. Press to complete a gnome hat.

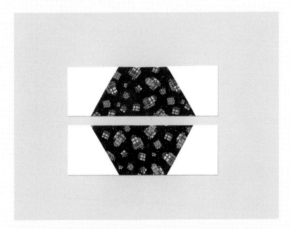

5 Sew 2 halves of half-hexagons to the angled sides of 2 matching half-hexagons. Press. Sew the 2 matching units together with the long sides of the half-hexagons touching. Press to complete a gnome body.

6 Sew a gnome hat to the top of a gnome body. Press toward the gnome body to complete the block.

1 **CHRISTMAS 1**

PALETTE

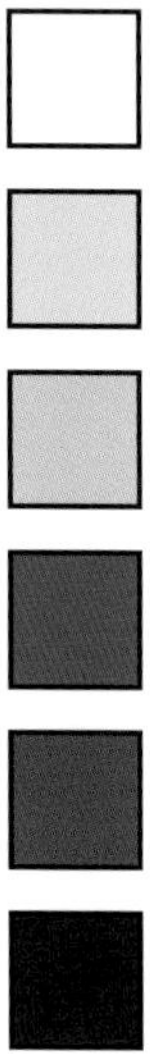

Bright packaging and the greenest tall tree make this wall hanging colorful and playful.

2 **CHRISTMAS 2**

PALETTE

For a subtle look that brings these gnomes home all winter long, our muted palette is softer but just as sweet!

GNOME PLACE LIKE HOME

Our seven stair-stepped (when they still did stair-step in age and height!)
In the back, our oldest, Darrell, then the girls left-to-right, Natalie, Sarah, and Hillary,
and the younger supermen in front, Al, Jake, and Josh.

Porch Quilts

CELEBRATE HOLIDAYS WITH QUILTS INSIDE AND OUT

There are a number of ways to display a quilt throughout your home, inside and out, that let your quilt flag fly! One way to let everyone know you have and love quilts is to put up a Porch Quilt. Jenny started this tradition and hangs quilts on her porch year round, especially during holidays and celebrations.

What is a porch quilt?

But just what is a porch quilt? Well, quite simply, it's a quilt that hangs on your porch. Porch quilts only look a bit tricky to get hung up for those new to them. Fortunately, Jenny and her helpful husband Ron show just how they get their quilts displayed on their porch. Jenny uses tension clips attached to a rod that is mounted to the porch ceiling. An alternative to these tension clips are decorative drapery clips, which can be found in any hardware store and are easy to use whether you are hanging the quilt by yourself or have an extra pair of hands.

- **1 MOUNT HOOKS OR CRADLES TO YOUR PORCH FRAME**

- **2 SLIP TENSION CLIPS OVER CURTAIN ROD**

- **3 CLIP QUILT TO CURTAIN ROD WITH TENSION CLIPS**

- **4 HANG ROD (AND QUILT!) FROM MOUNTED HOOKS**

There are a number of other ways to hang a quilt, too! If you know that the quilt you are making is going to be hung up on a porch, wall, or door at some point, you can also sew pockets into the corners or a sleeve at the top of the quilt to make hanging it easier. You might even use safety pins to attach a sleeve to your quilt and then hang it from a curtain rod on your porch, wall, or in a window!

**OPEN CAMERA. SCAN CODE.
WATCH JENNY & RON HANG
A PORCH QUILT.**

Hanging quilts without a porch

Maybe you don't have a porch at all? Take heart! There are still plenty of wonderful ways to gorgeously display any quilts you have in your home. First, check for porch-adjacent locations! Do you have a back, or side deck? Maybe a large open space beneath a window, or two? Do you live in an apartment building and have a balcony that overlooks a courtyard? All of these are great alternatives to a regular porch quilt that still expresses the spirit of flying your quilty flag to celebrate any holiday you love!

Here in Missouri, we love to see the quilts waving in the wind—but we do get weather, too! Porches are not the only way to hang your quilts, however, and many a beautiful quilt can be hung up almost anywhere for prominent display. One way is simply to hang it up in an empty wall space. It's true! You can hang any size quilt on the wall (it doesn't have to be a "wall hanging"—there are no quilt police!)

Hang any holiday quilt easily enough with just a handful of those drapery clips mentioned above, along with some heavier duty adhesive wall mounts or a curtain rod mounted to a wall (with or without a window!) You could use the same technique on any door in your house, even display a quilt on your front door, depending on the size of your quilt.

No rules for hanging quilts of all kinds

Speaking of quilt sizes, it's important to mention that there is no set size for any porch quilt, or for any quilt that you decide to display. Quilts come in all shapes and sizes, and all of them will fit nicely into any of the spaces mentioned, using any of the hanging methods provided. There is no such thing as a quilt that's too small for your porch, or too big for your living room. They're YOUR quilts, hang them wherever strikes your fancy!

Have fun with your holiday quilt displays. Maybe you'd like to organize and theme collections of quilts around a specific holiday, event, or celebration. Jenny had a lot of fun with a set of quilts to celebrate the 12 Days of Christmas and the end result was stunning. You could theme your display quilts after your own favorite holidays, and deck out your whole house in 4th of July, Valentine, Easter or Halloween themed quilts. Show your love of all the harvest colors all season long, or shine in the season of light with quilts that show a little more bright, cheerful joy as the days grow longer and nights grow shorter.

Porch quilts, along with any other kind of hanging display of quilts, are just a ton of fun, and can go a really long way to making your already beautiful home that much brighter and more colorful. The next time you're on your porch or inside your home looking at an empty space you'd like to fill, consider doing so with a gorgeous quilt that you've made yourself to celebrate your favorite holidays in your favorite colors!

PEPPARKAKOR COOKIES

Here's one you may have never heard of! Pepparkakor is a traditional Swedish cookie that's very similar to a gingerbread cookie and is a traditional favorite of our big Swedish family. You won't believe how delicious these thin, crispy cookies are!

INGREDIENTS

¾ Cup Shortening	1 Egg Beaten	1 Tsp each of Cloves, Cinnamon, and Ginger
1 Cup Sugar	2 Cups Flour	
1 tbsp Molasses	2 Tsp Baking Soda	

INSTRUCTIONS

Cream sugar and shortening together, add egg and molasses, blend well. Add the spices to the flour and sift, then add it to the creamed mixture. Let cool for 1 hour in the refrigerator covered with saran wrap. Then roll into balls the size of walnuts, put onto a cookie sheet, then with glass covered with saran wrap, roll each ball in sugar then flatten with the glass. Put nuts or raisins on them in the middle and bake at 350°F for 5-10 minutes or until golden brown.

Pepparkakor

3/4 cup Shortening
1 cup sugar
4 T Molasses
1 egg beaten
2 Cups of flour
2 tsp B. Soda
1 tsp each of Cloves, ginger
& Cinnamon.

Cream Shortening & sugar
together, add egg & Molasse.
Blend Well. Add the
spices to flour & sift
then add to creamed
Mixture. Let cool for
1 hour in fridge, Covered
with Saran m. Then
with a tsp pick up dough
& roll it into a ball
in your hands, have a
bowl with sugar & roll
ball the size of a Walnut
Put Saran m. over
a smooth Glass or Mug
First put the balls

DRINK SPECIAL
-Strawberry Lemonade
3.50
-Traditional Lemonade
3.00
1.50 Refills. -Pea_lmonade-4.00
-NEW-
-Mango Lemonade!-

Made in house
brine Picnics $4=

2 SPRING

Spring is a time of new beginnings and a cause for celebration in and of itself. There are many reasons to reawaken creativity after a long, chilly wintertime and these bright projects are sure to put a literal spring into your step! Invite plenty of color into your sewing room and feel the warmth wake you up and inspire you to start stitching. With life returning to the world around you and love in the air, what will you create? These beautiful projects are begging to be made and cherished for years to come.

INSIDE OUT HEART

Do you wear your heart on your sleeve? How about on a quilt? Create a cute inside out heart with this sweet pattern that's perfect to show you care. Start your project with a package of colorful 10" solid squares, add another package of 10" white squares for the heart, sew your half-square triangles, and your heart will skip a beat when you see the finished quilt!

MATERIALS

QUILT SIZE 36" x 36" | **BLOCK SIZE** 6½" unfinished, 6" finished

QUILT TOP

1 package of 10" solid squares in a variety of coordinating colors

1 package of 10" background squares - for the heart

BINDING

½ yard

BACKING

1¼ yards

OTHER

Clearly Perfect Slotted Trimmer A

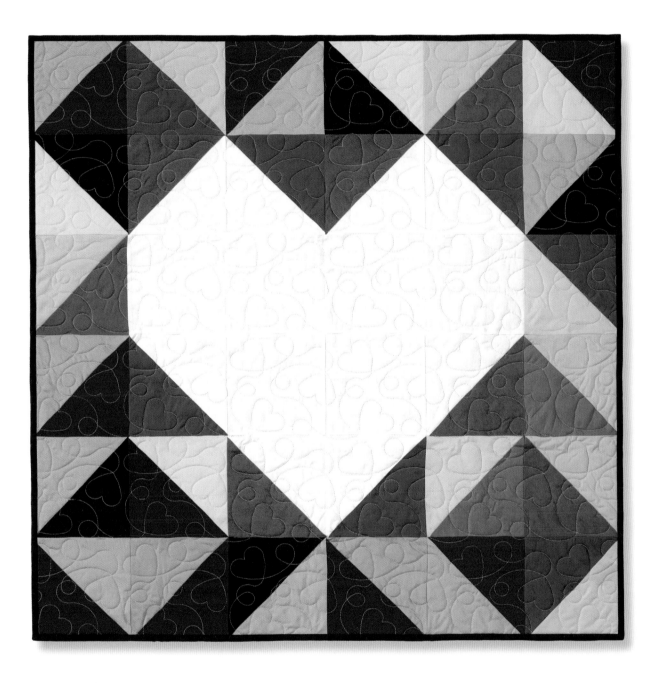

STEP: 1 cut

Select (6) 10″ background squares. Set the rest of the background squares aside for the moment. Trim the 6 squares to 6½″ and set them aside until you are ready to lay out the quilt top.

STEP 2: make the half-square triangles

Layer a 10″ background square right sides together with a solid square. Sew around the layered squares on all 4 sides using a ¼″ seam allowance. **2A**

Cut the sewn squares on both diagonals. Trim to 6½″ using the slotted trimmer. While you're in the process of trimming, use the slots provided to trim off the dog ears. Open and press toward the darker fabric. Note: Spray starching is recommended. Each pair of 10″ squares will yield 4 half-square triangles. Repeat with a second pair of 10″ squares to yield atotal of 8 background/solid half-square triangles. **2B**

Layer 2 different solid squares right sides together. Sew around the layered squares on all 4 sides using a ¼″ seam allowance. **2C**

Cut the sewn squares on both diagonals. Trim to 6½″ using the slotted trimmer. While you're in the process of trimming, use the slots provided to trim off the dog ears. Open and press toward the darker fabric. Each pair of 10″ squares will yield 4 half-square triangles. Repeat with 5 additional pairs of 10″ solid squares. You will need a **total of 22** solid/solid half-square triangles. Set the 2 extra half-square triangles and all remaining 10″ squares aside for another project. **2D**

Block Size: 6½″ unfinished, 6″ finished

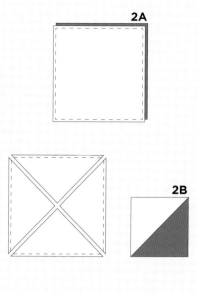

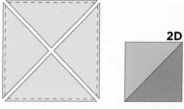
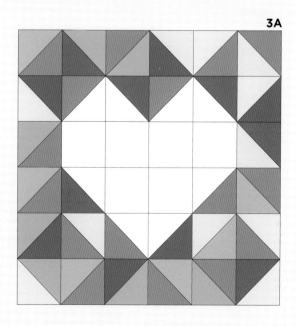

STEP 3: arrange & sew

Lay out the 6½″ background squares and blocks in **6 rows of 6**, making note of the location and orientation of the blocks in diagram **3A**. Sew the squares and blocks together to form rows and press in opposite directions. Nest the seams and sew the rows together. Press.

STEP 4: quilt & bind

Refer to the finishing sections of *How to Create a Quilt* on pages 12-14 to quilt, square and trim, then add binding to finish your quilt.

///////////////////////////////////// **MIX IT UP!** /////////////////////////////////////

1 HALLOWEEN

PALETTE

A playfully modern color palette for Halloween might add a range of purples and even a red or deep pink. Use the colors you love!

2 CHRISTMAS

PALETTE

A softer green/teal/pink is a modern spin on the traditional red and green Christmas Classic.

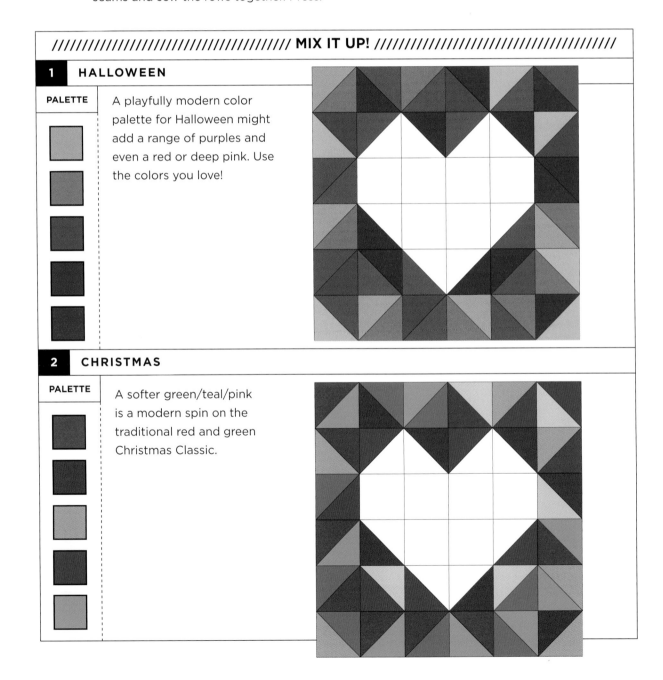

1 Layer a 10″ background square and a 10″ solid square together, right sides facing. Sew on all 4 sides using a ¼″ seam allowance.

2 Cut the sewn squares on both diagonals to yield 4 units.

3 Use the Clearly Perfect Slotted Trimmer A to trim each unit to 6½″.

4 Open each unit to reveal a half-square triangle. Press toward the darker fabric.

DRESDEN POUCH

We heart this handy pouch! Don't let the zipper make your heart pound, it's easy to install and

makes this bag oh-so-lovely. A sweet host/hostess gift all on its own, you'll also love to tuck a

little something inside!

MATERIALS

PROJECT SIZE
8½" x 9" finished

PROJECT SUPPLIES

4 - 8 assorted 5" print squares

(1) 5½" x 20" rectangle

(2) 2½" contrasting strips

(1) 9" x 20" rectangle of lining fabric

(1) 9" x 20" rectangle fusible fleece or batting

(1) 10" nylon zipper

Missouri Star Large Dresden Plate Template for 10" Squares

Note: You can make the bag any size you choose. The sizes of fabric given are just guidelines.

STEP 1: cut

From the 5″ squares, cut 8 blades using the template found on page 213. Align the 5″ mark on the template with the edge of a square. Cut 1, then flip the template 180° and cut another. **Note**: For a scrappier Dresden, use a different print square for each blade. **1A**

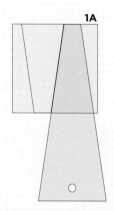

From the 2½″ contrasting strips:

- Cut (2) 2½″ x 20″ rectangles and (1) 2½″ x 5″ rectangle.
  - Trim the 2½″ x 5″ rectangle to a 1½″ x 5″ rectangle.

STEP 2: sew

Fold a wedge in half lengthwise with right sides together. Sew across the wide end, then clip the corner. Turn the point right side out. Press, centering the seam. **Make 8. 2A**

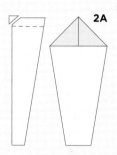

Sew the wedges together to make a Dresden fan. **2B**

Measure 5″ in from 1 edge of the 5½″ x 20″ rectangle. Mark that point with a pin, then place the center of the arc at the 5″ point and pin in place. The top of the half circle at the bottom of the Dresden will be meet the edge of the rectangle. **Note:** You will be trimming some of the bottom edges of the fan. **2C**

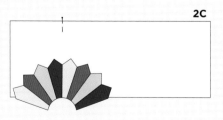

Use a blanket or zigzag stitch to appliqué the fan in place.

Remove the pin. Trim the arc evenly with the bottom of the rectangle. **2D**

Press the fusible fleece or batting to the reverse side of the lining fabric. Center the rectangle with the Dresden on top of the fleece, right side up. Align a 2½" x 20" contrasting strip along the top edge, right sides facing. Sew in place through all the layers.

Repeat for the remaining 2½" strip, stitching it to the bottom of the rectangle. Press the strips toward the outer edges of the fleece. Topstitch ¼" away from the seam lines. **2E**

Cut the rectangle in half vertically to **make (2)** 9" x 9½-10" rectangles to make the front and back of the pouch. Set aside while you prepare the zipper.

STEP 3: prepare the zipper

Fold the 1½" x 5" rectangle in half lengthwise, with wrong sides facing and press. Open and fold in the 2 long sides toward the center and press again. Cut the unit into (2) 1½" x 2½" zipper tabs. **3A**

Trim off the end of the zipper. Slide the zipper end into the fold of the tab. Topstitch through all three layers. Trim the tab even with the end of the zipper. **3B**

Lay the zipper along the top of the pouch. Slide back the zipper head so the zipper is open, then trim it so it is 1"

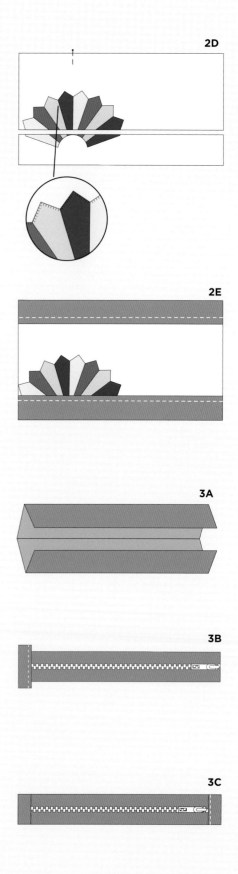

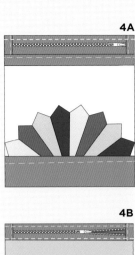

4A

4B

4C

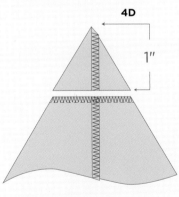

4D

1"

shorter than the opening of the bag. Slip the open ends of the zipper into the fold of the tab. Sew across the end of the tab in the same manner as before and, trim the ends of the tab even with the zipper. **3C**

STEP 4: finish pouch

Center the zipper face down on the edge of the right side of 1 of the pieces of the pouch. Stitch in place. As you approach the zipper pull, raise the presser foot of the sewing machine and slide the zipper pull down past the foot. Lower the presser foot and continue sewing to the end. **4A**

Fold the sewn edge of the zipper toward the inside of the bag and topstitch along the edge. Repeat the above instructions to install the zipper on the other side of the bag. **4B**

Open the zipper. Put the right sides of the bag together. Be sure the zipper stays open so you can turn the bag right side out. Sew just inside the ¼″ mark—down 1 side, across the bottom and up the remaining side. After you have sewn the seams, go back and use a zigzag stitch to finish the raw edges of the seams. **4C**

If you would like to have the bag to have a flat bottom, align the side seam of the bag with the bottom seam. Measure 1″ from the point of the peak and draw a line straight across. Sew on the drawn line, then trim the excess fabric away ¼″ from the sewn seam. Zigzag to finish the raw edges. Repeat for the other side of the bag. Turn the bag right side out. **4D**

1 │ Align the 5″ mark of the template with the edge of the 5″ square. Cut 1 blade. For 2 blades, move the template to 1 side, cut a blade, then rotate the template 180° and cut the second blade.

2 │ Fold each wedge in half with right sides facing. Sew across the widest part of the piece. Clip the sewn corner at a 45° angle.

3 │ Turn the point right side out. Press, centering the seam.

4 │ Sew 8 wedges together to make an arc. Pin the Dresden in place and stitch to the background fabric using zigzag or blanket stitch.

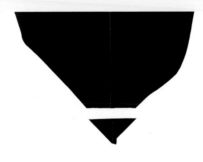

5 │ Open the bag, align the side seam of the bag with the bottom seam. Sew straight across about 1″ from the point. Trim the excess fabric ¼″ away from the sewn seam.

6 │ Turn the bag right side out.

/////////////////////////////////// **MIX IT UP!** ///////////////////////////////////

1 VALENTINES

PALETTE

The Valentines pouch can carry a multitude of sweet treats and sweeter love letters! For this pattern, we've chosen some gorgeous muted reds and pinks in marble prints that pair to form hearts in the Dresden fan.

2 THANKSGIVING

PALETTE

This handy, zippered pouch is not only a fantastic alternative to wrapping paper, but makes a handy handbag as well! Here we're using harvest colors with autumnal star and flower prints, along with alphabet prints on cream and auburn.

ZIGZAG PLACE MATS & NAPKINS

These simple squares sewn in diagonal rows make fast easy place mats (with coordinating fabric napkins!) for any and every season. For valentines with your own inner child, celebrate with fun vintage prints along with some pastel candy stripes and actual valentines cards! Whether it's pastels or softly muted coordinating colors, these are sew sweet!

MATERIALS

PLACEMAT SIZE 18⅜" x 12⅜" finished | **NAPKIN SIZE** 17" finished

NAPKIN SIZE

17" finished

PROJECT TOP

1 package of 5" print squares

BACKING

2¾ yards*

The backing fabric listed includes enough fabric for the backing of 4 place mats and to make 4 matching cloth napkins.

STEP 1: cut

Cut each 5″ square in half vertically and horizontally to yield 2½″ squares.

From the backing fabric, cut (2) 2½″ strips across the width of the fabric. Subcut (24) 2½″ squares from these strips and add these to the 2½″ print squares for a **total of 192** squares. Set the remaining backing fabric aside for now.

STEP 2: sort & sew

Separate the squares into 4 stacks of 48 squares each, distributing the colors or fabric prints amongst the stacks as you wish.

Lay out the 2½″ squares in diagonal rows as shown. **2A**

Sew the squares together to form diagonal rows. Press the seams in

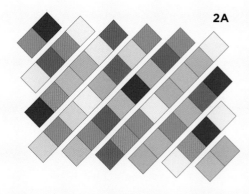

opposite directions. Nest the seams and sew the rows together to form a place mat top. Press. **Make 4. 2A**

STEP 3: finishing

From the backing fabric, cut (2) 24″ strips across the width of the fabric. Cut each strip in the middle to yield rectangles that measure approximately 24″ x 20″.

Lay a place mat top on a backing rectangle with right sides facing. Place the layered pieces atop a piece of batting, making sure the place mat is the top layer.

Stitch around the outer edge through all 3 layers, leaving an opening on 1 side for turning. **3A**

Trim the batting and backing evenly with the edges of the pieced top. Clip the corners and trim the points. Turn right side out. Press.

Stitch the opening closed and quilt as desired. **Make 4.**

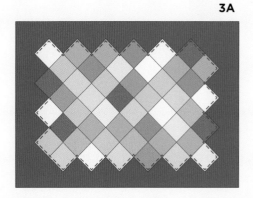

STEP 4: napkins

From the backing fabric, cut (2) 18″ strips across the width of the fabric. Subcut each strip into (2) 18″ squares.

Fold each edge in ¼″ towards the middle of the square with wrong sides together. Press.

Fold each edge of the square in ¼″ again to enclose the raw edges of the fabric within the fold. Press.

Topstitch around the edge to finish the napkin. **Make 4. 4A**

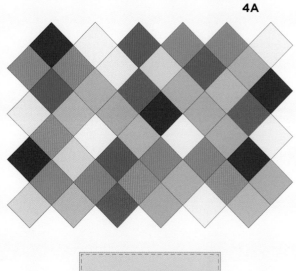

/////////////////////////////////// **MIX IT UP!** ///////////////////////////////////

1 VALENTINES B

PALETTE

Bold, rich burgundy, crimson, and just a touch of florals with pretty, soft blossoms on neutrals, and we've created an elegant, and romantic place setting.

2 CHRISTMAS

PALETTE

Sweet snowmen on bright red, candy canes on spearmint, and tiny wreaths on a soft white background create a holly, jolly, Christmas tablescape.

2 PATRIOTIC

PALETTE

Catch ketchup with these easy napkins and break out some star-spangled red, navy and bright white to create a classic, patriotic picnic feel. Absolutely perfect for any July 4th Celebration.

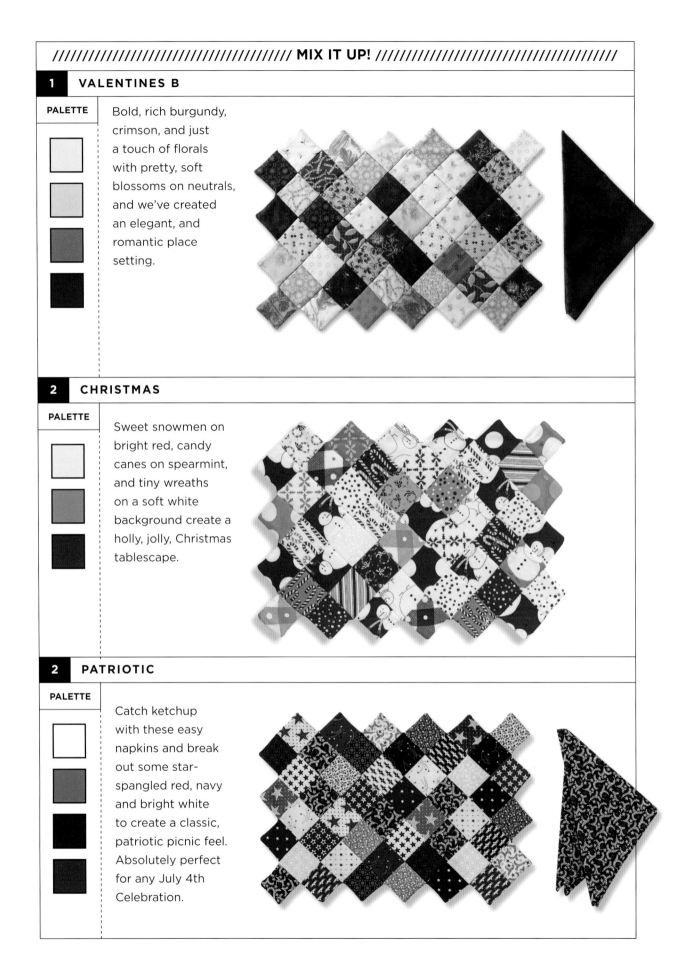

COME AS YOU ARE

VALENTINE'S DAY BREAKFAST DOAN STYLE

Jake and Misty's family enjoy a family favorite—Strawberry Cream Cheese Stuffed French Toast—with some sweet napkins to catch the crumbs!

Are you ready to have some fun with fabric? Let's talk about appliqué! Appliqué—or applying shaped patches of fabric to a background to form a picture or pattern—opens so many doors of what's possible when it comes to quiltmaking. No longer are you confined to basic shapes that can be achieved through patchwork like squares and triangles. A bat, a bunny, a horse? All doable thanks to appliqué!

The *Thankful Wall Hanging* (pg. 166) project calls for appliqué to add curved elements like scripted letters, turkeys, and pumpkins to a traditionally pieced quilt. The *Trick or Treat Street Table Runner* (pg. 150) is another project that combines piecing and appliqué for spooky bats and haunted houses that appear to fly off the quilt. If you are just getting started with appliqué, let me tell you that it is a fun and easy process to learn, and you'll be amazed at what you can create.

There are a few different methods of appliqué, some of which require a sewing machine and others that don't. The method we recommend most often to beginners is called "fusible appliqué", and we finish our edges on the sewing machine. We love using a fusible product to adhere fabric shapes to the quilt because it's fast, easy, and long-lasting through many washes. Ready to try your hand at fusible appliqué? There are a few supplies you'll want to have on hand before you get started.

Supplies

FABRIC & TEMPLATES

Appliqués can be cut from solid or print fabrics, and scraps are perfect for this! The appliqué patterns in this book also include the templates you can trace onto the paper side of a fusible product to make your own fabric shapes. **Tip:** Unless your shapes are all symmetrical, be sure to reverse the images before tracing them onto the fusible web (which adheres to the wrong side of the fabric). For your convenience, all of our templates are already reversed! It takes a little getting used to, but the first time you cut out a backward fabric shape on accident, you'll learn the lesson quickly!

FUSIBLE WEB (IRON-ON ADHESIVE)

What exactly is fusible web? In short, it's a thin layer of glue paper that gets pressed to the wrong side of two fabrics to adhere them together. Today's lightweight fusible webs are heat-activated and pressure-sensitive, so they will permanently affix fabrics when you use an iron and follow the manufacturer's instructions. For the appliqué projects in this book, you'll be pleased with a lightweight fusible web like Heat n Bond Lite or Missouri Star Sew Light Fusible Adhesive.

SCISSORS

For cutting around tight curves (think fabric letter appliqués), a pair of small, sharp scissors usually does the trick.

IRON & TEFLON PRESSING SHEET

An iron is what gives fusible web its magic powers. But make sure not to iron directly on top of fusible products unless you want your iron plate to become a sticky surface. We recommend using a special heat-resistant Teflon sheet to protect your iron from the adhesive that may wish to sneak out the sides of an appliqué patch and attach itself to your iron.

OPEN-TOE SEWING MACHINE FOOT

After adhering an appliqué to a quilt block, we like to use our sewing machine's open toe foot so nothing gets in the way of seeing my needle glide around the shape. It's often made of clear plastic so you can see what you're sewing with ease.

NEEDLE & THREAD

Speaking of needles, a Microtex 80/12 needle is my favorite choice for appliqué. The slim, sharp point pierces through densely woven fabrics with ease. A basic 50 weight cotton

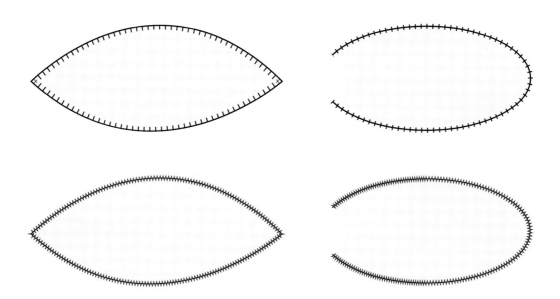

thread works well. If you want your thread to blend into the quilt, choose a thread color that matches the appliqué patch. Once you are more comfortable sewing around appliqués, you may want to change up the look of your stitch with a thicker 40 weight thread in a contrasting or variegated color.

WHAT THREAD COLOR SHOULD YOU PICK FOR APPLIQUÉ?
A THREAD THAT MATCHES YOUR DESIGN IS MORE FORGIVING
FOR THOSE JUST STARTING OUT.

Appliqué Tips & Tricks

WORKING WITH FUSIBLE WEB

Once your shapes are traced onto the paper side of the fusible web, you are ready to cut them out. But resist the urge to cut right on the line just yet! Use a small, sharp pair of scissors to cut ⅛" to ¼" around the outside of the shape. After you adhere it to the back of the fabric (following the manufacturer's directions), cut on the line for a nice, crisp edge on your appliqué.

Does your fusible refuse to stick? It may have gotten old and dried out. Next time, store your fusible in a resealable bag to keep it fresh. If your appliqués fall off of the quilt while you're working, you can easily tack them back down with a fabric glue stick.

CHOOSING A MACHINE STITCH

Two great appliqué stitches for beginners are a buttonhole stitch and a zig-zag stitch because you can easily work around a shape catching both the inside and outside of the

fabric patch. Choose a stitch width that allows a little space between your zigs and your zags, because this is easier to control than a dense satin stitch. Before you stitch your fused pieces of fabric down, test the stitch you'd like to use on a scrap piece of fabric. You can then adjust it to your liking. **Tip:** Make sure to write down the setting you like or take a picture of it with your phone, so you can use the same setting for all of the appliqués in your project.

START SEWING

Before you start sewing down the appliqués, pull enough thread out of your machine so you can hold on to your thread tails. Starting with the needle down on a straight edge (if possible), begin machine stitching around the shape. Keep in mind, your stitch should just barely hit the background fabric.

IT'S NOT A RACE

Ready to move around the shape? Stitch slowly and guide the project through the machine using both hands. It's okay to start and stop many times when you sew around a curve. Just take it nice and easy!

WHAT'S THE POINT?

When you're stitching toward a point, sew right up to the shape and put your needle down at the tip of the point to make sure it's sewn down completely. Then use the needle up/down function (or your machine's handwheel) to stop with the needle down. Lift the presser foot and gently pivot your quilt to continue sewing. Remember to always pivot when your needle is on the outside edge. If you pivot before, you'll create a v-shaped gap in the stitching. Continue sewing.

TIE OFF ENDS

When you're finished sewing around the appliqué, stop your machine and pull off some long thread tails before clipping the project off your machine. To bury your threads, thread a hand-sewing needle with both thread tails (self-threading needles work great), pull them through to the back of the quilt, and tie them off.

There you have it! Now that we've talked all about appliqué, we hope you have fun playing with fabric shapes in your projects. Feel free to come back here when you need a little refresher.

RON'S FAMOUS ECLAIRS

Delicious and easier than you might imagine to make right at home, Ron's famous eclairs are a hit at any Doan family gathering. It's always fun to watch who is daring enough to try and fit the entire eclair into their mouth. It definitely takes some skill! Whip these up for a special occasion and you'll be rewarded with plenty of oohs and aahs.

INGREDIENTS

PASTRY

½ Cup boiling water

½ Cup all purpose flour

¼ Cup butter

2 Eggs

Vanilla or chocolate Cook & Serve pudding

Sweetened whipped cream

FROSTING

¼ Cup butter

¼ Cup cocoa

½ Tsp vanilla

1½ Cup powdered sugar

3 Tbsp Cream

INSTRUCTIONS

Put the butter into a small saucepan and pour the boiling water over it. Heat it until it boils again. Add the flour and stir constantly until mixed well. Add eggs one at a time until the mixture becomes a smooth paste. Drop spoonfuls of the dough onto a cookie sheet or pipe into three inch long bars, six per sheet. Bake at 450°F for 15 minutes, then reduce heat to 300°F and bake for another 30 minutes. When cool, pierce a hole into the pastry and fill with vanilla or chocolate pudding and whipped cream. To make the frosting, cream the butter until it's soft and then add the sugar and cocoa alternately with the milk and vanilla. Blend thoroughly. Heat on low in a saucepan to darken. Frost the top and allow it to set. Enjoy!

3 SUMMER

These dazzling summer projects in patriotic colors are just what your family barbeque is calling for. Under the brilliant sun, the colors and patterns practically glow, taking on a life of their own. And just wait for twilight, when the fireworks burst and sparkle in the sky. It's an exciting time to celebrate the land we love and all the people who make it unique. Roll out a pretty picnic quilt, spread out all your favorite treats, and lie back to gaze up at the sunset. You just might catch a shooting star out of the corner of your eye.

ALL STARS

Patriotic prints make the background in this twist on the All Stars quilt, using a solid blue to form the stars. Flags, fireworks, denim blues and faded reds all come together to make this truly an All Star 4th of July quilt.

MATERIALS

QUILT SIZE 62½″ x 72″ | **STAR BLOCK** 10″ finished, 9½″ unfinished

HALF-STAR BLOCK 5″ x 10″ unfinished, 4½″ x 9½″ ufinished

QUARTER-STAR BLOCK 5″ unfinished, 4½″ finished

QUILT TOP	BORDER	BACKING
1 package of 10″ print squares	¾ yard	4½ yards - vertical seam(s)
1 roll of 2½″ background strips or 1¾ yards contrasting solid cut into (21) 2½″ width of fabric strips	**BINDING** ¾ yard	

STEP 1: cut

Select 21 strips from the roll. Cut each strip into (8) 2½″ x 5″ rectangles. A **total of 168** are needed. Set the remaining strips aside for another project.

STEP 2: block construction

Place a 2½″ x 5″ background rectangle atop 1 corner of a 10″ print square, on an angle, right sides facing. Position the rectangle so it will cover the corner once it has been pressed down. Sew in place, then press toward the outside edge of the square. **2A 2B**

Turn the block over and trim the excess fabric away evenly with the edge of the background square. **2C 2D**

Repeat for all 4 corners. Notice how all the narrow, pointed pieces are going in the same direction. Press. **Make 42. 2E**

Block Size: 10″ unfinished, 9½″ finished.

STEP 3: cut

Select 11 star blocks. Cut each in half to create 5″ x 10″ rectangles. **Make 22** half-star blocks and set them aside for the moment. **3A**

Block Size: 5″ x 10″ unfinished, 4½″ x 9½″ finished

Select 1 star block and cut it in half vertically and horizontally to **make 4** quarter-star blocks. Set these aside for the moment. **3B**

Block Size: 5″ unfinished, 4½″ finished

2A

2B

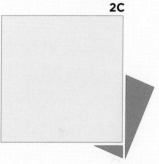

2C

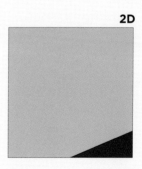

2D

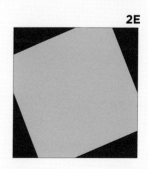

2E

STEP 4: arrange & sew

Arrange the blocks into rows as shown in diagram **4A**. Notice how each star is complete with all 4 points in place.

The top and bottom rows are made up of 5 half-star blocks and a quarter-star block on each end. **Make 2**. **4B**

The center rows are made up of 5 star blocks and a half-star block on each end. **Make 6**. **4C**

Sew the blocks together to form rows and press in opposite directions. Nest the seams and sew the rows together. Press.

STEP 5: border

Refer to diagram **5A** for the border. Cut (7) 3½" strips across the width of the fabric. Sew the strips together to make 1 long strip. Measure, cut, and attach the borders to the quilt top. The lengths are approximately 66½" for the sides and 63" for the top and bottom.

STEP 6: quilt & bind

Refer to the finishing sections of *How to Create a Quilt* on pages 12-14 to quilt, square and trim, then add binding to finish your quilt.

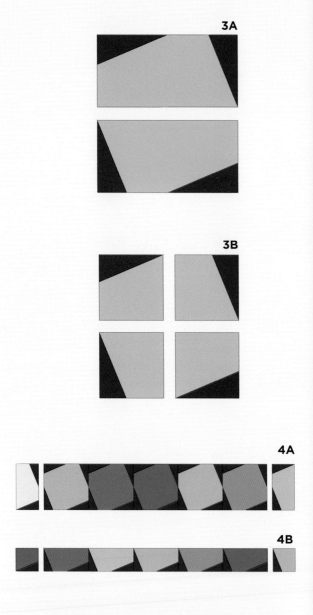

3A

3B

4A

4B

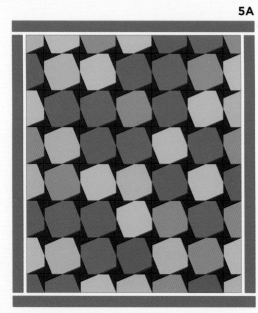

5A

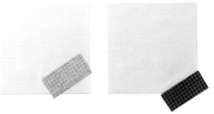
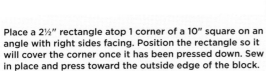

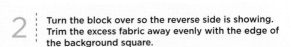

1 Place a 2½″ rectangle atop 1 corner of a 10″ square on an angle with right sides facing. Position the rectangle so it will cover the corner once it has been pressed down. Sew in place and press toward the outside edge of the block.

2 Turn the block over so the reverse side is showing. Trim the excess fabric away evenly with the edge of the background square.

3 Place the next rectangle on the next corner. Follow the directions above and stitch in place as before. Repeat for all 4 corners to complete 1 block. Notice how all the narrow, pointed pieces are going in the same direction. Make 42.

4 Select 11 blocks. Cut each in half to make 22 half-blocks.

5 Select 1 block and cut it in half vertically and horizontally to make 4 quarter-blocks.

/////////////////////////////// MIX IT UP! ///////////////////////////////

1 SUMMER

PALETTE

A deep, dark background, and some seriously vibrant colors take this pattern in a completely different direction, and show just how versatile the base pattern is when coupled with a creative eye. Our range of bright multi-colored stars almost sparkle. Switch up the prints and background fabrics to create a totally different look.

GEESE IN MOTION

When geese start to migrate in the fall, you'll want to get cozy with this magnificent quilt! It uses the Binding Tool to create an incredible flying geese herringbone pattern that's sure to impress. Soft garden-ready floral prints in pinks, teals, and yellows nestled in leafy greens give this such a Summer-in-bloom feel.

MATERIALS

PROJECT SIZE
73" x 70½"

QUILT TOP
1 roll of 2½" print strips

2 yards of background fabric

-includes sashing & inner border

OUTER BORDER
1¼ yards

BINDING
3/4 yard

BACKING
4½ yards - vertical seam(s) or 2¼ yards 108" width

OTHER
Binding Tool by TQM Products

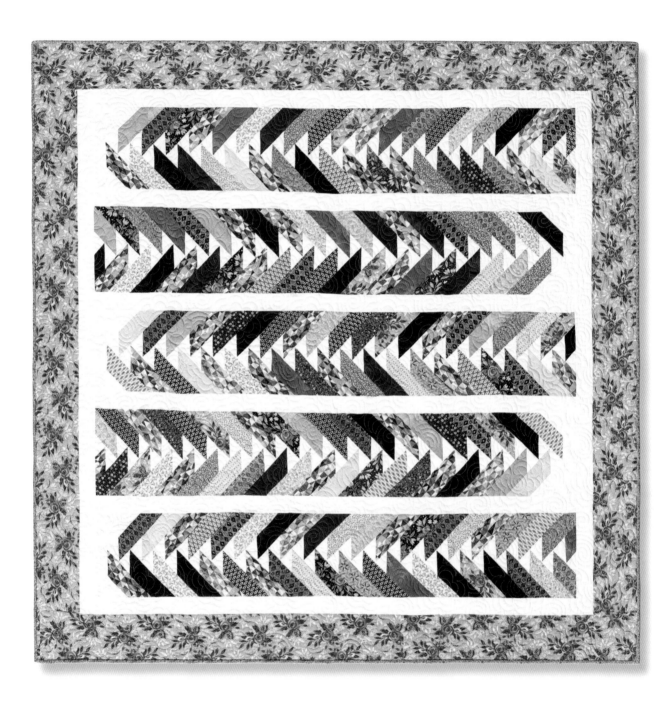

STEP 1: cut

Open the roll of print strips and leave each strip folded. Stack 2 to 4 strips atop each other and trim off the selvages. Align the blunt edge of the binding tool with the trimmed edge of the strips. Cut the angle through all layers. Turn the binding tool 180°, align the angled end with the cut edge, and again cut through all layers. Open the remaining portion of each strip—the piece that is still folded. Layer the strips with wrong sides facing and align the blunt edge of the binding tool with the end of the strips. Cut the angle. **1A 1B**

Separate the cut strips into stacks. Place all pieces that have the right side of the fabric facing up together. We'll call these A pieces for the sake of clarity. Place all the pieces that have the fabric facing down into another stack which we will call B pieces. Notice how the A pieces and B pieces are mirror images of each other. There will be a **total of 100** A pieces and a **total of 100** B pieces in each stack. **1C**

From the background fabric, cut:

- (25) 2½″ strips across the width of the fabric.
  - Subcut a **total of (203)** 2½″ squares from 13 strips.
    - Cut (3) 2½″ squares once on the diagonal to **make (6)** 2½″ triangles.
  - Set the remaining 12 strips aside for the sashing strips and inner border.

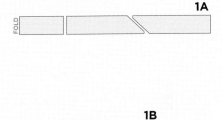

1A

1B

1C

A B

- (1) 6½" strip across the width of the fabric.
  - Subcut (3) 6½" squares and (3) 5" squares.
    - Cut each square once on the diagonal to **make (6)** 6½" triangles and **make (6)** 5" triangles.

STEP 2: snowball the A & B pieces

Mark a diagonal line on the reverse side of each 2½" background square. **2A**

Place a marked square, right sides facing, on the blunt end of each A and B piece. Notice the orientation of the diagonals of each marked square. **2B**

Sew on the marked line. Trim away the excess fabric ¼" from the sewn seam. Press toward the outer edge of the strip. Stack all A pieces together and all B pieces together. **2C 2D**

STEP 3: build the horizontal rows

Select (1) 2½" background triangle, 20 A pieces and 20 B pieces. Align the snowballed end of an A piece with 1 edge of the triangle, right sides facing. Sew the triangle in place as shown. Open and press. **3A 3B**

Add a B piece to the end of the unit as shown. Press. **3C**

Continue alternating the A and B pieces until you have made a braided row using the 20 A pieces and 20 B pieces. Press. **3D**

Pick up a 5" triangle and sew it to the B side of the row with right sides facing. Open and press. **3E 3F**

Stitch a 6½" triangle to the A side of the strip with right sides facing. Open and press. **3G 3H**

Square up the opposite end of the row by trimming it flush with the bottom of the triangle with which you began the row initially. **Make 5** rows. **3I**

STEP 4: make horizontal sashing

Pick up 9 of the 2½" background strips you set aside earlier. Sew the strips together to make 1 long strip. Cut the sashing rectangles from the strip. Measure the width of your rows and cut your sashing strips to that measurement, approximately 58½". A **total of 6** strips are needed.

Refer to diagram **4A** on page 136 and lay out the rows. Notice rows 2 and 4 are oriented differently than rows 1, 3, and 5. Sew the rows together with a sashing strip between each row. Add a sashing strip to the top and bottom as well. Press.

STEP 5: inner border

Pick up the 3 remaining 2½" background strips that were set aside earlier. Sew the 3 strips together to make 1 long strip. Trim the 2 side borders from this strip. Measure, cut, and attach the inner borders to the quilt top. Each strip should measure approximately 60".

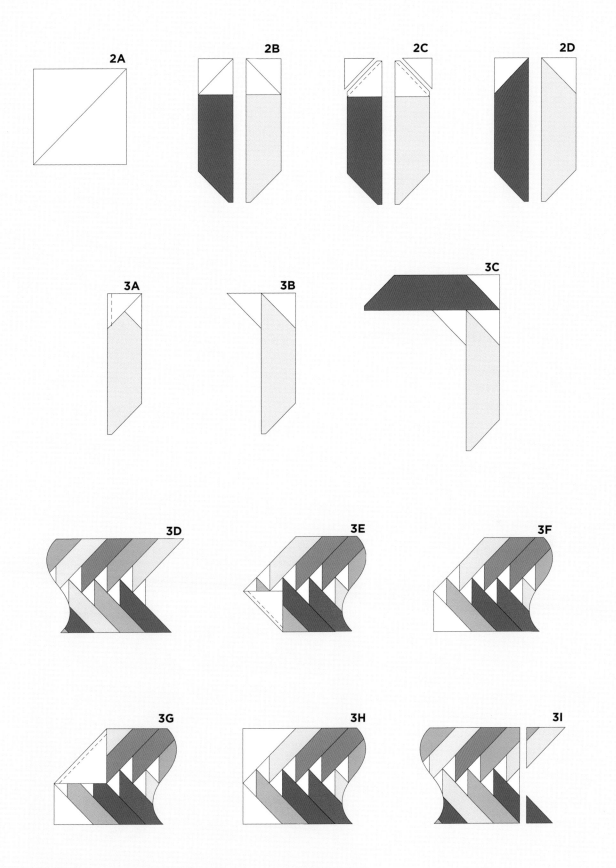

STEP 6: outer border

Cut (7) 6″ strips across the width of the fabric. Sew the strips together to make 1 long strip. Trim the borders from this strip. Measure, cut, and attach the outer borders to the quilt top. The lengths are approximately 60″ for the sides and 73½″ for the top and bottom.

STEP 7: quilt & bind

Refer to the finishing sections of *How to Create a Quilt* on pages 12-14 to quilt, square and trim, then add binding to finish your quilt.

4A

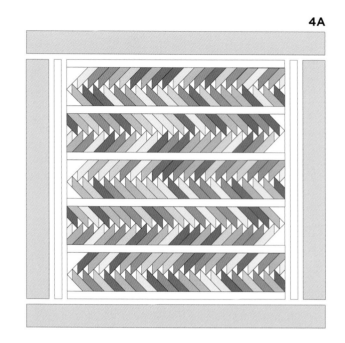

/////////////////////////////////// **MIX IT UP!** ///////////////////////////////////

1 | **CHRISTMAS**

PALETTE

Christmas in July or winter brights, the greens, whites and reds in this Geese in Motion quilt give it a ribbons and wrapping paper feel. Traditional fabrics and colors make this instantly recognizable as a Christmas quilt!

1 Place a marked background square on the blunt end of an A and B piece making sure the marked line is not parallel to the cut angle of the print piece. Sew on the marked line and trim away the excess fabric. Repeat with all remaining A and B pieces.

2 Press toward the background fabric.

3 Place a 2½" background triangle right sides together with an A piece. Sew the pieces together along the edge of the triangle.

4 Press the triangle away from the A piece.

5 Add a B piece to the other side of the triangle and stitch in place. Open and press.

6 Continue adding on additional pieces until you have a total of 20 A pieces and 20 B pieces forming a row. Make 5 rows.

CHARM QUILT & PILLOW ON POINT

Say hello to easy! Create this charming quilt by simply sewing 5" squares into rows. Then make two quick cuts, rearrange, stitch them back together, and an enchanting new look appears like magic! Use the same idea to make a coordinating pillow—some clever stitching and it's all on point!

QUILT MATERIALS

QUILT SIZE
57¾" x 57¾"

QUILT TOP	**OUTER BORDER**	**BACKING**
2 packages of 5" print squares	1¼ yards	3¾ yards - vertical seam(s)
INNER BORDER	**BINDING**	
½ yard	¾ yard	

PILLOW MATERIALS

PILLOW SIZE
19" x 19"

PROJECT TOP
1 package of 5" print squares

Fiberfill

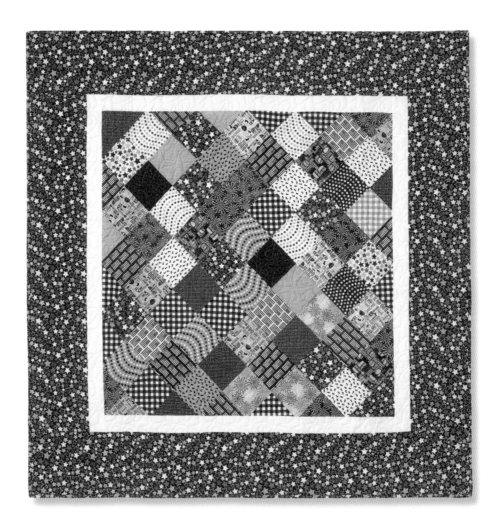

For the Quilt

STEP 1: sew

Sew the 5″ print squares into **12 rows of 6.** While sewing the blocks together, mix up the color values so the lights, mediums, and darks are spread out rather than all grouped together. **1A**

Press the rows in opposite directions. Nest the seams and sew the rows together to make 1 large rectangle.

STEP 2: mark & cut

Align a ruler with the upper right corner and the lower left corner of the bottom of the 6th row of squares. Make sure the ruler is intersecting the corner of each block. Cut on the diagonal, being careful not to stretch or tug on the edges.

Without moving the project, realign the ruler with the top of the first square on the left side of row 7 and the bottom of the last square on the right in row 12. Again, make sure the ruler is intersecting the corner of each block. Carefully cut on the diagonal. **2A**

Number each section and draw an arrow beside the number so you can keep track of which direction each section is oriented. Refer to the diagram and notice how the sections are numbered. **2B**

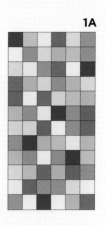

STEP 3: rearrange & sew

Pick up Section 3 and place it to the right of Section 1. Make sure the arrows still point in the same direction as before. Pick up Section 2 and place it under Section 3. Refer to diagram **3A**

Sew Section 3 and Section 2 together horizontally. Press the seam allowances toward Section 2.

Add Section 1 to the left and sew in place after making sure all block seam allowances are aligned.

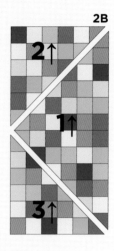

STEP 4: inner border

Refer to diagram 4A below for the inner and outer borders. Cut (5) 2½" strips across the width of the fabric. Sew the strips together to make 1 long strip. Measure, cut, and attach the inner borders to the quilt top. The lengths are approximately 39¼" for the sides and 43¼" for the top and bottom.

STEP 5: outer border

Cut (5) 8" strips across the width of the fabric. Sew the strips together to make 1 long strip. Measure, cut, and attach the outer borders to the quilt top. The lengths are approximately 43¼" for the sides and 58¼" for the top and bottom.

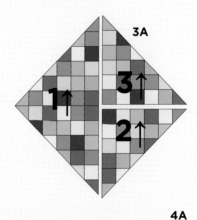

STEP 6: quilt & bind

Refer to the finishing sections of *How to Create a Quilt* on pages 12-14 to quilt, square and trim, then add binding to finish your quilt.

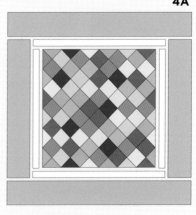

141

For the Pillow

STEP 1: arrange & sew

Select 36 print squares for your pillow and set the remaining squares aside for another project. Arrange the squares into **6 rows of 6** as shown. The middle 4 squares will be the center of 1 side of the pillow and the 4 corner squares will make up the center of the other side. Sew the squares into 6 rows. Press the seams of the odd-numbered rows toward the right and the seams of the even-numbered rows toward the left. Nest the seams and sew the rows together to make a 27½" pieced square. Press the seams toward the bottom. **1A**

Fold the pieced square in half, right sides together. Stitch the short ends closed, backstitching at the beginning and end. **1B 1C**

Bring the 2 side seams you just stitched together and match them up. Poke out the corners. Stitch the open seam together

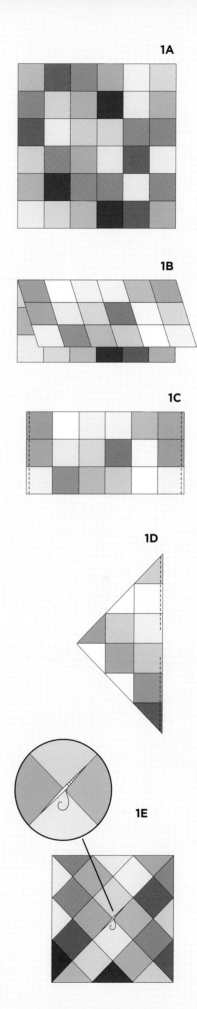

1A

1B

1C

1D

1E

beginning at 1 end. Backstitch and then sew approximately 12″ and backstitch again. Remove the unit from under the sewing machine foot. Turn the unit and start sewing the open seam closed from the other end. Backstitch at the beginning and stop when you have an opening that is about 4″ and backstitch. **1D**

Clip the corners of the seams to reduce the bulk and turn the pillow right side out and fill with the Fiberfill. Once it is filled to your satisfaction, sew the opening closed using a ladder stitch or a whipstitch. **1E**

FRONT

BACK

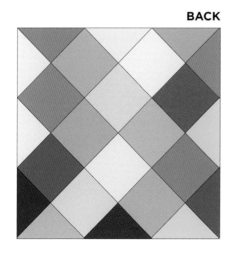

//////////////////////////////////// **MIX IT UP!** //

1 PATRIOTIC

PALETTE

The softer side of sparklers, add razzle and dazzle with stars and more stars in a range of denim blues and bright reds.

2 CHRISTMAS

PALETTE

We're all about the Christmas Cards and the prints in this collection are addressing our letters to Santa.

RED, WHITE, AND VROOM!

Ron and the boys on bikes for our 4th of July dirt bike soccer game.
We'll be having a picnic style feast soon!

MISTY'S CHICKEN HOT WING DIP

The Fourth of July is always a fun time here in Hamilton. A love for our country is deep in our hearts and our main street is filled with waving flags. There are many beloved family traditions surrounding this holiday and they make it even more exciting. Just before it's time to light up the sky with fireworks, we put out a big BBQ spread and it always includes this incredibly delicious chicken hot wing dip. Enjoy!

INGREDIENTS

2 cups cooked, shredded chicken breast	½ cup hot wing sauce	Tortilla chips
	½ cup ranch dressing	Celery sticks
1 8 oz. package softened cream cheese	1 cup grated mozzarella or cheddar cheese	

INSTRUCTIONS

Heat oven to 350°F degrees. Mix all ingredients together and pour into an 8" x 8" oven-proof dish. Bake for 30 minutes until it's melted and bubbly. This dip can also be heated up in a Crock Pot. Serve with tortilla chips and celery sticks.

4 FALL

When the winds change and a cool autumn breeze blows, a feeling of anticipation is in the air. The holiday season begins with beautiful changing leaves, flurries of early snow, and plenty of quilting. It's the perfect time to head back into the sewing room after soaking up the summer sun. Start stitching with fun and playful Halloween projects for kids and adults alike. Then, create your own Thanksgiving decorations with plenty of time before family arrives for the festivities. Everyone will adore sitting down to a cozy table filled with your thoughtful handmade creations.

TRICK OR TREAT STREET TABLE RUNNER

Stitch up a boo-tiful table runner for your Halloween soirée! This cute Trick or Treat Street pattern is filled with fun appliqué details that make each house unique along with flying bats to set a spooky scene. Choose fabric styles that make your heart go thump in the night and sew by the light of a full moon!

MATERIALS

PROJECT SIZE
40" x 30"

BLOCK SIZE
10½" unfinished,
10" finished

PROJECT TOP
1 package 5" print squares

½ yard yellow solid fabric
- includes inner border

½ yard gray background fabric

OUTER BORDER
¾ yard

BINDING
½ yard

BACKING
1 yard

OTHER
Missouri Star Large Dresden Plate Template for 10" squares

½ yard fusible web

STEP 1: cut

From the gray background fabric, cut (2) 10½″ strips across the width of the fabric. Subcut (6) 10½″ squares. Set the remaining fabric aside for another project.

From the yellow solid fabric, cut (1) 6″ strip. Set the remaining fabric aside for the inner border.

STEP 2: make houses

Note: You can vary the number of 6″, 5″, and 4″ tall houses for your project. You just need a **total of 30** Dresden houses. Have fun and make it your own!

Lay the 6″ yellow strip on your cutting surface horizontally. Place the Dresden template found on page 213 on top of the strip as shown, lining up the 2½″ mark of the template with the bottom edge of the strip. **2A**

Carefully cut along both sides of the template. **2B**

Turn the template 180°, lining up the left edges and the 2½″ mark of the template with the top of the strip. Cut another

Dresden. Continue in this fashion to cut a **total of 5** yellow Dresdens from the strip. Set the remaining piece of the strip aside for the appliqué shapes. **2C**

Select (25) 5″ print squares with varying prints to use for houses.

Stack as many squares on your cutting surface as you feel comfortable cutting at 1 time and align all edges. Lay the template along 1 side of the squares and line up the 2½″ mark of the template with the bottom edge of the squares. Carefully cut along both sides of the template. Cut a **total of (13)** 5″ print Dresdens. Set the scraps aside for the appliqué shapes. **2D**

Trim 1″ from the top of each of the 12 remaining squares. The 1″ strip can be set aside for the appliqué windows. Repeat the previous instructions to cut a **total of (12)** 4″ print Dresdens from the trimmed squares. **2E**

Select (2) 4″ and (2) 5″ Dresdens of varying prints. Add 1 yellow Dresden and arrange so there are Dresdens of different heights next to each other. When you are pleased with your arrangement, sew the Dresdens together using a ¼″ seam allowance. The small end of the Dresdens should always be lined up. Press the seam allowances toward the tallest Dresdens. Where the top edges of the tallest Dresdens extend past the shorter Dresdens, turn the raw edges under ¼″ and press. **2F**

Lay the Dresden unit atop a 10½″ background square as shown. Pin in place. **2G**

Repeat the previous steps to **make 6** blocks. **Note:** 1 block will have 5 print Dresdens and no yellow Dresden.

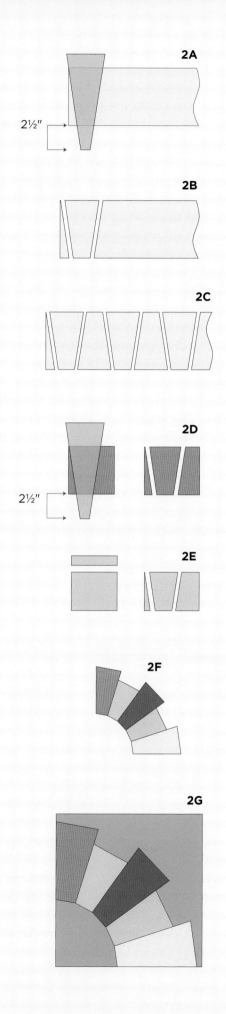

153

STEP 3: appliqué windows & doors

Note: The templates we used to create the bats, roofs, doors, and windows can be found on pages 214 and 215. The template shapes are meant to be a starting point. Feel free to modify them to your liking or create your own shapes.

For each appliqué shape needed, trace the appropriate template onto the paper side of your fusible web. Roughly cut around the traced line, then follow the manufacturer's instructions to adhere the fusible web to the reverse side of your fabric. Use the remaining 5" print squares and any leftover pieces set aside earlier to create your shapes. Once the fusible web has adhered, carefully cut along the traced line. Peel off the paper backing and discard it.

Note: For this step, you will be appliquéing doors and windows only. The roofs and bats will be appliquéd after the borders are added.

Once you have prepared each of the shapes needed for your block, lay them out on top of the block. Make any modifications or adjustments you like. Do not place windows or doors within the ¼" seam allowance along the outer edges. When you're happy with the arrangement, follow the manufacturer's instructions to adhere the shapes to the block.

After all of the appliqué windows and doors have been fused to the block, stitch around the edges of the appliqué shapes and along the bottom edge of the houses with a blanket or zigzag stitch. **3A**

Block Size: 10½" unfinished, 10" finished

STEP 4: arrange & sew

Referring to diagram **4A**, lay out your blocks in **2 rows** of **3 blocks** each. Pay special attention to the orientation of the blocks. Sew the blocks together in rows. Press the seam allowances of the top row to the left and the bottom row to the right. Nest the seams and sew the rows together. Press the seam towards the bottom.

STEP 5: inner border

Refer to **7A** below for the inner and outer borders. Cut (3) 1½" strips across the width of the yellow solid fabric. Trim the borders from these strips. Measure, cut, and attach the inner borders to the project top. The lengths are approximately 30½" for the top and bottom and 22½" for the sides. **Note:** The top and bottom strips are sewn on first, followed by the side strips for this project.

STEP 6: outer border

Cut (4) 4½" strips across the width of the outer border fabric. Trim the borders from this strip. Measure, cut, and attach the outer borders to the project top. The lengths are approximately 32½" for the top and bottom and 30½" for the sides. **Note:** The top and bottom strips are sewn on first, followed by the side strips for this project.

STEP 7: appliqué roofs & bats

Following the instructions outlined in section 3—trace, fuse, and cut out the

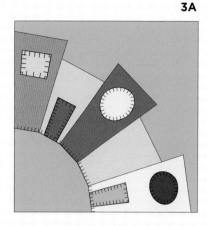

3A

shapes needed for your roofs and bats from fabrics that will provide contrast to the borders and the houses to which they are applied.

Referring to the diagram **7A** as needed, lay the shapes on top of your project top. Make any modifications or adjustments you like. When you're happy with the arrangement, follow the manufacturer's instructions to adhere the shapes to the project top.

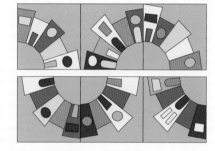

4A

After all of the appliqué shapes have been fused to the top, stitch around any remaining raw edges of your project with a blanket or zigzag stitch.

STEP 8: quilt & bind

Refer to the finishing sections of *How to Create a Quilt* on pages 12-14 to quilt, square and trim, then add binding to finish your project.

7A

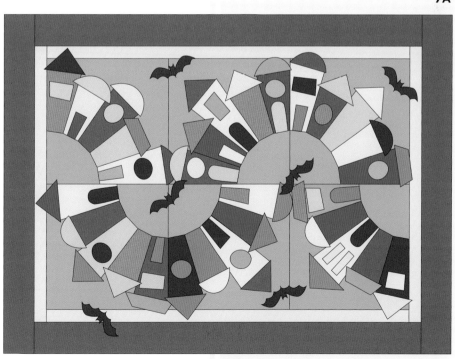

1 Line up the 2½" mark of the template with the bottom edge of the 6" yellow solid strip. Cut along both sides of the template. Turn the template 180°, line up the left edges and the 2½" mark of the template with the top of the strip, and cut another Dresden. Repeat to make 5 yellow Dresdens.

2 Lay the template along 1 side of the 5" squares and line up the 2½" mark of the template with the bottom edge of the squares. Carefully cut along both sides of the template. Cut (13) 5" print Dresdens.

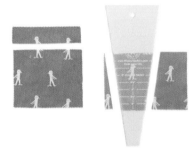

3 Trim 1" from the top of each of 12 print squares. Repeat the previous instructions to cut (12) 4" print Dresdens from the trimmed squares.

4 Arrange 1 yellow Dresden, (2) 4" Dresdens, and (2) 5" Dresdens so there are different heights next to each other. Sew them together using a ¼" seam allowance, aligning the small ends. Press toward the tallest Dresdens and turn any remaining raw edges under ¼" and press.

5 Lay the Dresden unit atop a 10½" background square and pin in place.

6 Arrange and adhere the doors and windows, then stitch around the edges of the appliqué shapes and along the bottom edge of the houses with a blanket or zigzag stitch.

/////////////////////////////////// **MIX IT UP!** ///////////////////////////////////

1 | HALLOWEEN

PALETTE

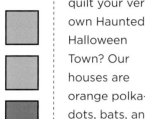

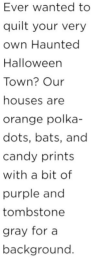

Ever wanted to quilt your very own Haunted Halloween Town? Our houses are orange polka-dots, bats, and candy prints with a bit of purple and tombstone gray for a background.

2 | CHRISTMAS

PALETTE

One big circle creates this Christmas Village, alternating houses and Christmas trees! This sweet little town would be a great table topper for your gingerbread house! We left out a few houses to make room for some evergreens. Find the templates for the tree and star on page 214.

CANDY CATCHER BAG

Surprise the little ones in your life with a Halloween bag that will hold all the goodies they can possibly pick up during their rounds of trick or treating! No kids? No worries, make one for yourself and carry it as a purse!

MATERIALS

PROJECT SIZE
13½" x 15"

SUPPLIES		
1 package of 5" print squares	¾ yard of contrasting fabric – includes lining and strap	25" x 40" scrap of lightweight batting

STEP 1: outer bag

Select (21) 5″ print squares. Sew the squares into **7 rows of 3**. Sew the rows together to form a rectangle. Set aside the remaining squares for another project. (It's the perfect amount to make a second bag!) **1A**

Cut a piece of batting—4″ wider and 4″ longer than the pieced rectangle. Place the pieced rectangle on top of the batting and quilt, using any design you like. Trim and square up the edges, approximately 14″ x 32″.

Lay out the quilted and pieced rectangle on the lining fabric and cut a rectangle the same width and length.

Fold the pieced and quilted rectangle in half lengthwise, right sides facing. Sew the side seams together. After the side seams are sewn, make boxed corners by pulling on 1 corner of the bag until a peak is formed. Measure 1¾″ from the point of the peak and draw a line straight across. Sew on the drawn line, then trim the excess fabric away ¼″ from the sewn seam. Repeat for the other corner of the bag. **1B**

STEP 2: lining

Fold the lining rectangle in half lengthwise with right sides facing. Sew the side seams together leaving an opening of about 4″ in 1 seam. Be sure to take a couple of back stitches on both sides of the opening. **2A**

Follow the directions in Section 1 to make the boxed corners in the lining. Set the 2 pieces of the bag aside for the moment while you make the strap.

STEP 3: strap

Cut (1) 1½″ x 40″ strip of lightweight batting.

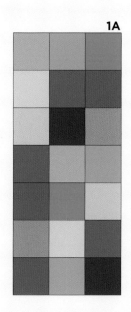

1A

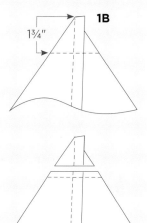

1¾″ **1B**

2A

Cut (1) 5″ x 40″ contrasting fabric strip. Trim the selvages and fold the strip in half lengthwise with wrong sides facing. Press. Open the strap and press both raw edges in ¼″ toward the center crease. **3A**

Open 1 of the folded edges and place the 1½″ strip of batting between the center of the strip and the fold. **3B**

Fold the strip in half along the center pressed crease and stitch the strap closed by sewing ¼″ from the edge. Add 2 more lines of stitching by sewing ¼″ in from the opposite edge and right down the center. Trim the ends of the strap to your desired length. **3B**

Turn the body of the bag inside out. Place the strap inside. Center 1 end of the strap to the side seam on 1 side of the bag and pin in place. Repeat for the other end of the strap, and pin to the remaining side seam.

Turn the lining right side out. Drop it into the bag—notice that the right sides are facing each other. Align the side seams and pin in place through all 3 layers (lining, bag, and strap). Pin the lining to the bag in several more places. Start on a side seam and sew all the way around the top using a seam allowance a bit wider than ¼″. **3C**

Reach into the bag and find the opening that was left in the side seam of the lining. Pull the whole bag through the opening to turn it right side out. After turning, whipstitch the opening in the lining closed and tuck inside the bag. Top stitch around the top about ¼″ from the edge to complete the bag.

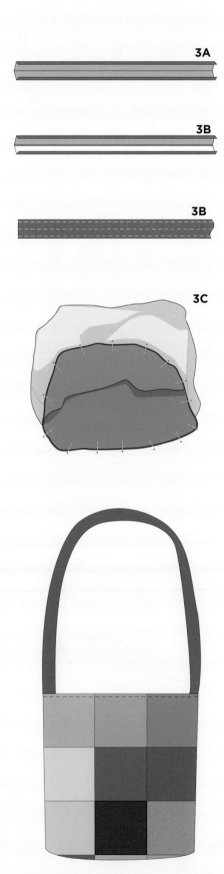

3A

3B

3B

3C

1   Sew (3) 5″ squares together to make a row. Make 7 rows and sew the rows together to form a rectangle.

2   Place the pieced rectangle on top of the piece of batting and quilt as you like. Trim the excess batting away and square up the edges of the rectangle.

3   Cut a 5″ x 40″ Contrasting fabric strip. Fold the strip in half and press with wrong sides together. Fold the raw edges in toward the center and press. Slip a 1¼″ x 40″ strip of batting in under one fold.

4   Fold the strap in half along the center pressed crease and stitch the strap closed by sewing ¼″ from the edge. Add 2 more lines of stitching by sewing ¼″ in from the opposite edge and right down the center. Trim the ends of the strap to your desired length.

5   After the side seams are sewn, make boxed corners by pulling on 1 corner of the bag until a peak is formed. Measure 1¾″ from the point of the peak and draw a line straight across. Sew on the drawn line, then trim the excess fabric away ¼″ from the sewn seam. Repeat for the other corner of the bag.

1 SPRING

PALETTE

Collect eggs on Easter, or carry a stack of your favorite books to the park. Nothing says spring like bright golden flowers! We used this collection of yellows and bright blues for a fun bag you can use all Spring long.

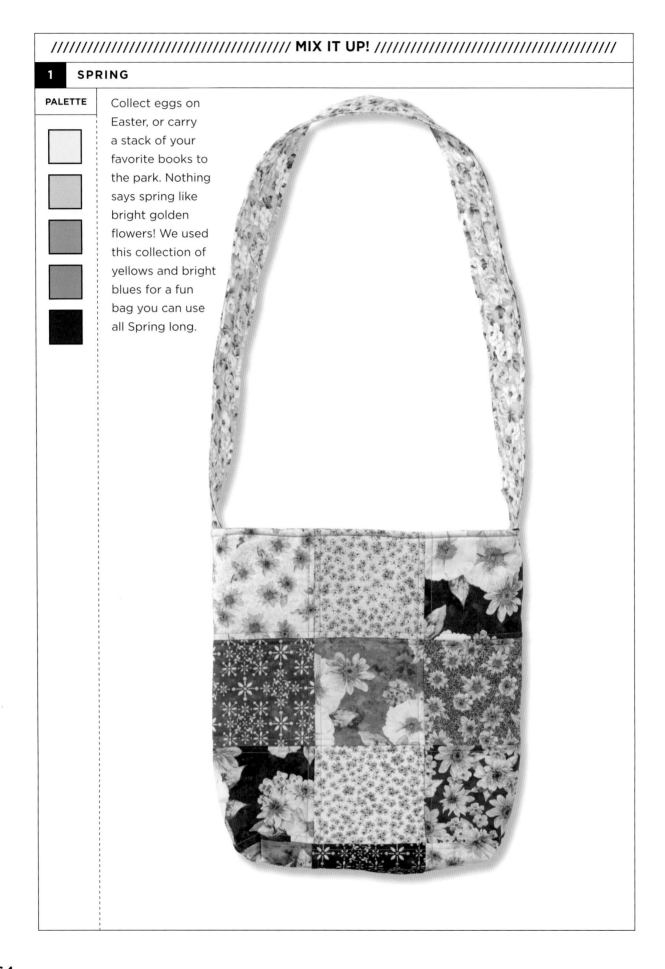

COSTUMES ARE A LOVE LANGUAGE

Before I was a quilter, I sewed costumes. Lots of costumes.
Our family gets into Halloween costumes in a big way. We have a feast of themed foods
and snuggle under spooky quilts when there's a chill in the air.
We all dress up as characters we love and we never forget to take a photo!

THANKFUL WALL HANGING

These cute Dresden turkeys are all dressed up and ready to celebrate. Add a full harvest moon,

plump little pumpkins, fall leaves, and flying geese for an autumn wallhanging that's perfect

for the entire season.

MATERIALS

PROJECT SIZE 42" x 40½" | **FLYING GEESE BLOCKS** 4½" x 2⅝" unfinished, 4" x 2⅛" finished
PUMPKIN BLOCKS 5" unfinished, 4½" finished | **LEAF BLOCKS** 6½" unfinished, 6" finished
MOON & CLOUDS BLOCKS 9½" unfinished, 9" finished
SMALL TURKEYS 9½" unfinished, 9" finished | **LARGE TURKEY** 14" unfinished, 13½" finished
THANKFUL BLOCK 20½" x 9½" unfinished, 20" x 9" finished

QUILT TOP

2 packages of 5" print squares

¾ yard of black solid fabric

¾ yard of gold print fabric

¾ yard of background fabric

BORDER

¾ yard

BINDING

½ yard

BACKING

2¾ yards – horizontal seam(s)

OTHER

Missouri Star Large Dresden Plate Template for 10" squares

1¼ yards Heat n Bond Lite

- -

Note: Separate the tan print squares in your packages from the rest of the 5″ print squares. These tan squares will be used as background fabrics.

STEP 1: thankful appliqué

Cut

From the background fabric, cut a 9½″ strip across the width of the fabric. Subcut a 20½″ x 9½″ rectangle from the strip. Set the remainder aside.

From the black solid fabric, cut a 6″ strip across the width of the fabric.

From the fusible web, cut a 20½″ strip across the width. Subcut a 6″ x 20½″ rectangle and set the rest of the fusible web aside.

Trace & Fuse

Trace the Thankful template on pages 216 and 217 onto the paper side of the fusible web.

Lay the black solid fabric on your pressing surface. Lay the fusible web with the traced letters on top of the fabric with the glue side touching the wrong side of the fabric. Adhere the fusible web to the fabric following the manufacturer's instructions. Cut out along the traced lines. Peel the paper backing off and discard it.

Lay the background fabric right side up on your pressing surface. Lay the appliqué letters right side up on top of the background fabric, centering it within the background rectangle. When you're happy with the placement of the appliqué, follow the manufacturer's instructions and adhere the shape to the background fabric.

Appliqué

Stitch around the edges of the fused fabric using a blanket or small zigzag stitch to complete the block. Set aside. **1A**

Block Size: 20½″ x 9½″ unfinished, 20″ x 9″ finished

STEP 2: moon & clouds

Cut

Pick up the remainder of the 9½″ background strip used in the previous section. Subcut a 9½″ square from the strip and set the remainder aside.

From the gold fabric, cut an 8″ strip across the width of the fabric. Subcut an 8″ square from the strip and set the rest of the fabric aside for another project.

Pick up the remainder of the 20½″ strip of fusible web used in the previous section. Subcut (1) 7½″ square, (1) 2½″ x 6″ rectangle, and (1) 3″ x 7″ rectangle. Set any excess fusible web aside.

Trace & Fuse

Trace the Moon on page 219 onto the paper side of the 7½″ square of fusible web.

Lay the 8″ gold square wrong side up on your pressing surface. Lay the fusible web with the traced moon on top with the glue side touching the wrong side of the fabric. Adhere the fusible web to the fabric following the manufacturer's instructions. Set aside for the moment.

Using the templates found on page 216, trace Cloud #1 onto the paper side of the 2½″ x 5″ rectangle and Cloud #2 onto the 3″ x 6″ rectangle.

Lay (2) 5″ black print squares wrong side up on your pressing surface. Lay the 2 rectangles of fusible web with the traced clouds on top with the glue side touching the wrong side of the fabric. **Note**: The fusible web rectangles will need to be placed on a 45° to fit on the 5″ fabric squares. Adhere the fusible web to the fabric following the manufacturer's instructions.

Cut out the moon and clouds along the traced lines. Peel the paper backing off the appliqué shapes and discard it.

Lay the 9½″ background square right side up on your pressing surface. Lay the appliqué pieces right side up on top of the background fabric, positioning them so the moon is roughly centered in the background square and the clouds do not overhang into the ¼″ seam allowances. When you're happy with the placement of the appliqué pieces, follow the manufacturer's instructions and adhere the appliqué pieces to the background fabric.

1A

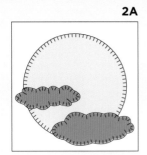

2A

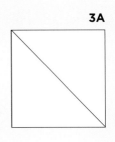

3A

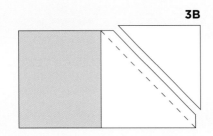

3B

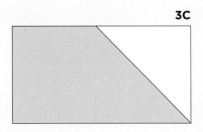

3C

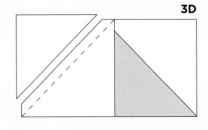

3D

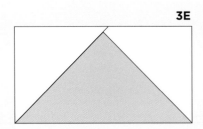

3E

4A

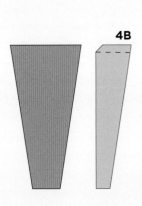

4B

4C

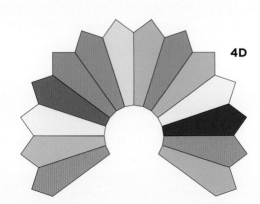

4D

Appliqué

Stitch around the edges of the fused fabric using a blanket or small zigzag stitch to complete the block. Set aside. **2A**

Block Size: 9½″ unfinished, 9″ finished

STEP 3: flying geese

Cut

Select (7) 5″ print squares from your package. From each square, cut a 4½″ x 2⅝″ rectangles for a **total of 7** rectangles.

From the background fabric, cut a 2⅝″ strip across the width of the fabric. Subcut (14) 2⅝″ squares from the strip and set the remainder of the strip aside for another project.

Sew

Draw a diagonal line on the reverse side of each background square. Lay a background square atop a print rectangle with right sides facing and the right edges aligned. Sew on the marked diagonal line. Trim the excess fabric ¼″ away from the seam and press. **3A 3B 3C**

Place another background square on top of the unit with right sides facing and the left edges aligned. Sew on the marked diagonal line. Trim the excess fabric ¼″ away from the seam and press. Notice that the seams overlap at the top of the block. **3D 3E**

Make 7. Set the blocks aside.

Block Size: 4½″ x 2⅝″ unfinished, 4″ x 2⅛″ finished

STEP 4: large turkey

Cut

From the background fabric, cut a 14″ strip across the width of the fabric. Subcut (1) 14″ square and set the remainder of the strip aside.

Select (14) 5″ print squares to use for the turkey's tail feathers. Cut each square in half to yield (28) 2½″ x 5″ rectangles. Separate the rectangles into 2 piles of 14 rectangles each. Set 1 pile aside to use for the small turkeys' feathers later. Use the Dresden Template found on page 213 to subcut the remaining pile into large feathers. Lay the 5″ marking on the template on top of the short edge of a rectangle and subcut along both sides. A **total of 14** large feathers are needed. **4A**

From the fusible web, cut a 5″ strip across the width. Subcut (1) 5″ square, (1) 3¼″ x 5″ rectangle, (1) 3¼″ square, and (1) 1″ square.

Sew

Fold each feather in half lengthwise, with right sides facing. Stitch straight across the larger end using a ¼″ seam allowance. **4B**

Trim the corner, open the seam and turn the point right side out. Press, centering the seam. **Make 14. 4C**

Join the 14 feathers to make a turkey tail. Begin sewing at the top of the feather and stop at the bottom. Be sure to backstitch at the top of the feather and press all seams to 1 side. **4D**

Lightly press the background square in half vertically to make a placement line. Use the crease as a guide to place the turkey tail on the background square about 1¾″ down from the top. Pin in place. Appliqué the turkey tail to the background square using a blanket or small zigzag stitch. **4E**

Trace & Fuse

Using the templates found on pages 217 and 218 trace the Turkey Body template onto the paper side of the 5″ square of fusible web. Trace the Large Turkey Head onto the 3¼″ x 5″ rectangle, the Large Turkey Legs onto the 3¼″ square, and the Large Turkey Beak onto the 1″ square. Roughly cut around the shapes as needed to prevent any fusible web overhanging the fabric and adhering to your pressing surface.

Select (3) 5″ print squares to use for the turkey and lay them wrong side up on your pressing surface. Lay the traced shapes onto the desired fabrics with glue side touching the wrong side of the fabric. Adhere the fusible web to the fabric following the manufacturer's instructions. Cut the shapes on the traced lines. Peel off the paper backing and discard.

Lay the background square with the tail feathers attached right side up on your pressing surface. Lay the Turkey Body piece on top of the tail feathers making sure to cover the circular void in the tail feathers. Set the Large Turkey Head on top making sure it extends a little bit below the bottom of the Turkey Body. Slide the Large Turkey Feet underneath the bottom edge of the Large Turkey Head and place the Large Turkey Beak on top. Once you're happy with the placement of each

of the pieces, follow the manufacturer's instructions to adhere them to your block.

Appliqué

Stitch around the edges of the fused fabric using a blanket or small zigzag stitch to complete the block. Set aside. **4F**

Block Size: 14″ unfinished, 13½″ finished

STEP 5: pumpkins

Cut

Cut a 4″ strip across the width of the fusible web. Subcut (1) 3″ x 4″ rectangle, (1) 4″ square, (1) 3¼″ x 4″ rectangle, and (3) 1½″ squares from the strip.

Trace & Fuse

Using the templates found on pages 218 and 219, trace Pumpkin #1 onto the paper side of the 3″ x 4″ rectangle of fusible web. Trace Pumpkin #2 onto the 4″ square. Trace Pumpkin #3 onto the 3¼″ x 4″ rectangle. Trace Stems #1, 2, and 3 onto the 1½″ squares.

Lay (4) 5″ print squares from your package wrong side up on your pressing surface. Lay the traced shapes onto the desired fabrics with the glue side touching the wrong side of the fabric. Each pumpkin shape will take most of a 5″ square, but you will be able to fit all of the stems on 1 square. Adhere the fusible web pieces to the fabric following the manufacturer's instructions. Cut the shapes on the traced lines. Peel off the paper backing and discard.

Select 3 of the 5″ tan print squares you set aside in the beginning. Lay these right side up on your pressing surface. Lay a pumpkin right side up on top of each tan background square. Slide a stem underneath the pumpkin. When you're happy with the placement of the pieces adhere the shapes to the background squares.

Appliqué

Stitch around the edges of the fused fabric using a blanket or small zigzag stitch to complete the block. Set aside. **Make 3. 5A**

Block Size: 5″ unfinished, 4½″ finished

STEP 6: small turkeys

Cut

From the remainder of the 14″ background strip cut when making the Large Turkey block, cut a 9½″ x 14″ rectangle and set the rest of the strip aside. Trim the 9½″ x 14″ rectangle to 9½″ square and set the excess fabric aside for another project.

Pick up the leftover pile of (14) 2½″ x 5″ rectangles you sat aside earlier when making the Large Turkey block. Use the Dresden Template (pg. 213) to subcut each of these rectangles into 3 small feathers. Lay the 2½″ marking on the template on top of a long edge of a rectangle and subcut along both sides. Rotate the template 180° and cut another feather. Rotate the template 180° another time to cut a third feather. A **total of 42** small feathers are needed. **6A**

From the fusible web, cut a 5″ strip across the width. Subcut (3) 5″ squares and (3) 1″ square.

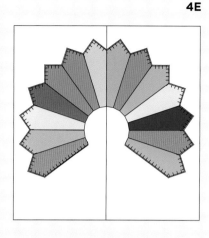

4E

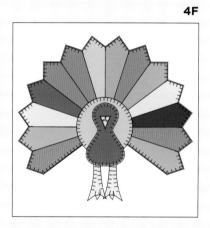

4F

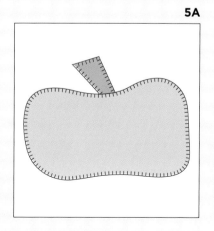

5A

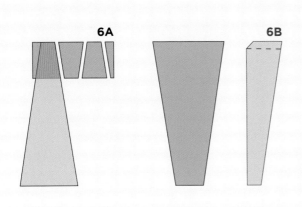

6A **6B**

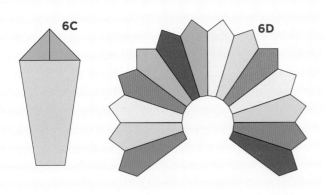

6C **6D**

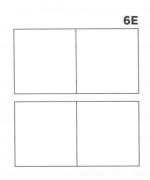

6E

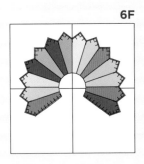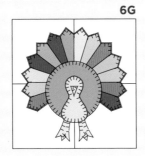

6F **6G**

Cut a 4″ strip across the width of the fusible web. Subcut (3) 2½″ x 4″ rectangles and (3) 2½″ x 4″ rectangles. Set the remainder of the fusible web aside.

Sew

Fold each feather in half lengthwise, with right sides facing. Stitch straight across the larger end using a ¼″ seam allowance. **6B**

Trim the corner, open the seam and turn the point right side out. Press, centering the seam. **Make 42. 6C**

Join 14 feathers to make a turkey tail. Begin sewing at the top of the feather and stop at the bottom. Be sure to backstitch at the top of the feather and press all seams to 1 side. **Make 3. 6D**

Select (8) 5″ tan background squares and sew them together in pairs and press to 1 side. Nest the seams and sew together in a 4-patch formation to make the background to be used for 2 small turkey blocks. Make 2. **6E**

Use the seams on the 4-patch as a guide to place the turkey tail on the 4-patch about 1½″ down from the top. Pin in place. Appliqué the turkey tail to the 4-patch using a blanket or small zigzag stitch. **Make 2. 6F**

Fold the 9½″ background square in half vertically and horizontally, then crease. Notice how the creased lines are in the same place as the seam lines of the 4-patches. Appliqué the last turkey to the creased background square similar to the other 2.

Trace & Fuse

Using the templates found on page 218, trace the Turkey Body onto the paper side of each 5″ square of fusible web. Trace the Small Turkey Head onto each 2½″ x 4″ rectangle, the Small Turkey Legs onto each 2¾″ x 4″ rectangle, and the Small Turkey Beak onto each 1″ square. Roughly cut around the shapes as needed to prevent any fusible web overhanging the fabric and adhering to your pressing surface.

Select (8) 5″ print squares to use for the turkeys and lay them wrong side up on your pressing surface. Lay the traced shapes onto the desired fabrics with glue side touching the wrong side of the fabric. Each Turkey Body and Small Turkey Head will take most of a 5″ square, but you will be able to fit multiple of the other shapes on the same square. Adhere the fusible web pieces to the fabric following the manufacturer's instructions. Cut the shapes on the traced lines. Peel off the paper backing and discard.

Lay an in-progress block right side up on your pressing surface. Lay a Turkey Body on top of the tail feathers making sure to cover the circular void in the tail feathers. Set the Small Turkey Head on top and then slide a pair of Small Turkey Feet underneath the bottom edge of the Small Turkey Head and place the Small Turkey Beak on top. Once you're happy with the placement of each of the pieces, follow the manufacturer's instructions to adhere them to your block.

Appliqué
Stitch around the edges of the fused fabric using a blanket or small zigzag stitch to complete the block. Set aside. **Make 3. 6G**

Block Size: 9½″ unfinished, 9″ finished

STEP 7: leaf blocks

Cut
Select 8 of the 5″ tan print squares set aside in the beginning and cut each square in half vertically and horizontally to make 2½″ squares. Each square will yield 4 squares and a **total of 30** are needed. Set the remaining 2 squares aside for another project.

Select (12) 5″ print squares. Choose 2 of these squares to use for the stems. Cut (3) 1½″ x 4″ rectangles from both of the selected 5″ print squares. You will need a **total of 5** rectangles for the stems.

Cut each of the remaining 10 print squares you selected in half vertically and horizontally to make 2½″ squares. Each square will yield 4 squares. Keep the matching prints together.

Make Stem Units
Choose a 1½″ x 4″ rectangle and a 2½″ background square. Press the square in half on the diagonal. Press the rectangle in half lengthwise with wrong sides facing. Open the pressed square and align the long raw edges of the pressed rectangle along the crease on the right side of the background square. Stitch the rectangle to the background square using a ¼″ seam allowance. Fold the rectangle back over, covering the seam allowance and topstitch along the pressed edge. Trim the edges of the rectangle even with the square to complete the stem unit. **Make 5. 7A**

Make Half-Square Triangle Units
Select 2 sets of 4 matching 2½″ print squares that coordinate well with each other and (5) 2½″ background squares. Draw a diagonal line on the reverse side of 4 of the background squares. Choose 4 of your print squares to use for the half-square triangles in the leaf block.

Note: We chose to make some of the blocks using the same print in all 4 half-square triangles and some are a combination of the 2 prints used in each block.

Note: You were instructed to select a **total of 8** matching 2½″ print squares to make each block, but only 7 of these will be used. You can set the remaining 2½" square you selected aside for another project after you have decided on the fabric placement within your block.

Place a marked background square atop a print square and sew on the marked line. Trim the excess fabric ¼" away from the sewn seam. Open and press the seam allowance toward the darker fabric. **Make 4. 7B**

Block Construction

Lay out the half-square triangle units, 1 stem unit, 1 background square, and 3 of your remaining selected 2½" print squares in rows as shown. Set the remaining 2½" print square aside for another project. **7C**

Sew the pieces together to make 3 rows, then sew the rows together to complete 1 leaf block.

Make 5 and set blocks aside. **7D**

Block Size: 6½" unfinished, 6" finished

STEP 8: arrange & sew

Cut

From the black solid fabric, cut (3) 1½" strips across the width of the fabric. Subcut (1) 1½" x 14" rectangle, (1) 1½" x 16" rectangle, and (1) 1½" x 9½" rectangle from 2 of the strips. Subcut (1) 1½" x 9½" rectangle from the third strip. Set the remainder of the strip aside for another project.

From the border fabric, cut (1) 5" strip across the width of the fabric. Subcut (1) 5" x 2½" rectangle and (1) 6" x 5" rectangle. Trim the 5" x 6" rectangle to 4" x 6".

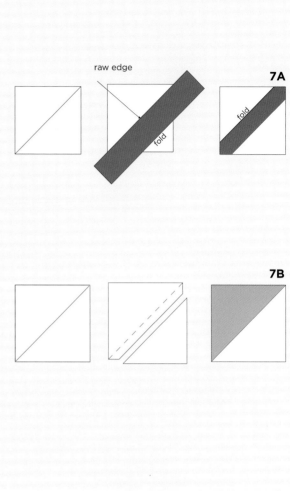

7A

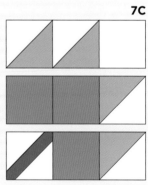

7B

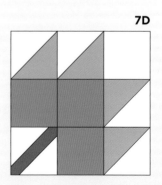

7C

7D

8A

8B

8C

8D

Cut (1) 3″ strip across the width of the fabric. Subcut (2) 3″ x 15″ rectangles.

Sew

Sew the Thankful block to the left side of the Moon & Clouds block. Press to complete the top row. **8A**

Sew the 7 flying geese together in a vertical row with all geese pointing up and using a seam allowance a thread or 2 wider than ¼″. Adjust your seam allowance between blocks as necessary so that the vertical row measures 15″ from top to bottom. Press toward the bottom of the row. Sew a 3″ x 15″ border rectangle to each side of the vertical row of flying geese. Press toward the border rectangles. Sew the 1½″ x 9½″ black solid rectangle to the top of the flying geese. Press.

Sew a 1½″ x 14″ black solid rectangle to each side of the large turkey block. Press toward the dark fabric. Sew a 1½″ x 16″ black solid rectangle to the top and bottom of the large turkey block. Press toward the dark fabric.

Sew the 3 pumpkin blocks in a vertical row. Sew the 2½″ x 5″ border rectangle to the bottom of the vertical row. Press.

Sew the flying geese to the left side of the large turkey block. Press. Sew the pumpkins to the left side of the large turkey block. Press to complete the middle row. **8B**

Arrange the 3 small turkey blocks in a row and separate them with the 1½″ x 9½″ black solid rectangles. Sew and press toward the darker fabric to complete the bottom row. **8C**

Sew the 3 rows together. Press. **8D**

8E

9A

Sew the leaf blocks together in a vertical row with all stems pointing toward the bottom left corner. Press. Sew the 4" x 6" border rectangle to the bottom of the row. Press. Sew the vertical row to left side of the quilt top. Press. **8E**

STEP 9: borders

Refer to diagram **9A** for the border. Cut (4) 4" strips across the width of the fabric. Sew the strips together to make 1 long strip. Trim the borders from this strip. Measure, cut, and attach the borders to the project top. The lengths are approximately 34" for the sides and 42½" for the top and bottom.

STEP 10: quilt & bind

Refer to the finishing sections of *How to Create a Quilt* on pages 12-14 to quilt, square and trim, then add binding to finish your quilt.

MISSOURI LIFE
M
MISSOURI STAR QUILT CO.

GATHERING AROUND THE TABLE

Whether it was a birthday or a holiday, we always gathered around the table,
thankful for each other and the happiness in our life.
Left-to-right, Sarah, Jake, Alan, Hillary, and Natalie in a candid moment
that still makes this mama smile.

Creating Traditions

& MAKING HANDMADE MEMORIES

Do you want to create a brand new tradition of your own, but aren't sure where to start? Have you ever wanted to use your quilts and quilting skills to decorate your home around the holidays? Maybe you want to add some new messes, er, memories to your holidays! All it takes is a little creativity, some gusto, and the desire to create beautiful things. All of which any quilter has in spades!

Why Do You Love Your Traditions?

Before we get into creating new traditions, let's talk about some that you already celebrate. What are some holiday habits that you share with your family and friends? Is a particular feast or snack your favorite? Maybe a shared trip home or away? Or a simple group activity, like singing carols, playing games, or watching a movie? Why do you love these traditions? What is it about them that makes you happy? Is it the food itself, setting the table, or is it the sharing of closely-guarded family recipes? Is it the destination or the journey—or is it simply the fact that you are with the ones that you love? The answers to all of these questions can be really important to any new traditions you might want to create.

Making Something New

Speaking of new traditions, making something new isn't just for the quilts and projects we make—it's for how we use them, too. Relationships are constantly growing and shifting. We take on new roles in our families and friend groups and you can often find yourself invited to new celebrations or even creating new traditions entirely. Maybe you'll find one of these quilty ideas inspires you to build your own version with your loved ones!

One tradition we started with our big, beautiful family is a quilt raffle of sorts. For the last few holidays, I've crafted a beautiful quilt, wrapped it up, and then put all of our family's names into a hat. Whoever's name is pulled from the hat gets the quilt! How about that for a new tradition? Any project from this book could be a fun project to share this way—from the bigger quilts to wrap up in (we do love all our Missouri Star Quiltss! page 20) or picnic

on (try *Charm Quilt on Point*, page 138) to the fun, fast pillows or sweet bags. Who wouldn't love to win the holiday raffle?

So how do you start a new tradition? Is it as simple as coming up with an activity and then deciding to do it again periodically? Well...it sure can be! It can be as simple as writing a message on a tablecloth or as involved as passing a quilt from one family member to another, changing hands every New Year's Day. Make a friend or family member a quilt for their bbq picnic under the stars, hang a porch quilt to signal the trick or treaters—just go ahead and start a tradition. Give yourself the permission to do so, and just do it. Once you've started making memories, all that's left is to intentionally repeat it the next year and tada! You've started a tradition. Go YOU!

Traditions Can Be Gifts, Too

Not every quilting tradition needs be the quilting or giving of larger, bed-sized quilts. You can make small projects that create sweet, thoughtful gifts to pass your love on to others. The *Candy Catcher Bag* (page 158) is a handy, fun and fast project perfect for trick-or-treating or egg-collecting kiddos. The stylish *Dresden Pouch* (page 100) is just big enough to carry a couple of jars of jam or a lovely fragrant candle and can go on to serve as a pretty little handbag. *Zigzag Place Mats & Napkins* (page 108) are an easy to customize project that is also quite practical for any table and any season. All of these can serve as wonderful host/ hostess gifts when visiting friends and family or when sending your love across the many miles to them when you can't be there in person.

Make Memories and Take Pictures!

Whatever projects you choose to create your traditions, take lost of photos of them! Take a snap shot of you hanging up your first porch quilt (page 86) or wall hanging. Set your tables with all of your runners, mats, napkins and make memories with the place settings, centerpieces, and favorite foods. Take photos of the quilts all over your house from the throws on your couch, to the runners on your bed. Take pictures of your family staying warm and snug while using your quilts. Take pictures of quilts that you plan to gift to loved ones

and pictures of the quilts you love so much that you can't bear to even consider letting them go. Take as many pictures of your quilt-work as you can, because in doing so, you are creating even MORE memories, memories that you can then share with others, even if the quilts themselves aren't with you.

Quilting doesn't just create a finished product; it also creates a handmade memory. The quilts and other projects you complete not only possess the memories you've made in creating them, but also the memories you make using them, giving them, snuggling under them and feasting over them. Friends, family, even those who receive your beautiful, generously donated items all create their own beautiful memories handmade in your stitches, your patchwork, and your love. In turn, these memories can spawn traditions that last years, decades, and beyond. In this way, your small acts of creativity, no matter how imperfect, can grow into generations of memory and tradition. Go. Make. Your world is waiting for the quilter that is you.

SEASONS - LIGHT, RENEWAL, AND HARVEST

Many traditions are associated with holidays, but some can be associated with a whole season. The season of Pumpkin Spice seems to bring in autumn colors, harvest flavors, and cozy style. Spring starts a thaw into early flowers, rain showers, and the season of renewal. The Season of Light itself begins just as Halloween is ending, and is full to the brim with holidays and traditions. As the days grow longer and darker extending through Diwali, Hanukkah, Kwanzaa, Yule, and of course Christmas, there is a wealth of wonderful inspiration to draw from and fit any pattern you see in these pages to the holidays you celebrate. Whether your traditions are filled with the bright, eye catching colors of spring in blossom, or the calm, somber, subdued shades of a winter morning after a snowstorm, there is inspiration here for you.

7 LAYER DIP

Layers of luscious sour cream, guacamole, and beans with all our favorite taco toppings make this dip a hit for practically any holiday! If you're feeling festive, pipe a cute sour cream spider's web on top to make it spooky for your Halloween party. No matter how you dress it up, this classic 7 Layer Dip is sure to be a hit with your friends and family. And don't forget to have plenty of chips on hand!

INGREDIENTS

1 package taco seasoning

1 (16 ounce) can refried beans

1 (16 ounce) container sour cream

1 (8 ounce) jar salsa

1 large tomato, chopped

Ready made Guacamole

1 (6 ounce) can sliced black olives, drained

2 cups shredded Cheddar cheese

1 plastic spider

INSTRUCTIONS

In a medium bowl, combine the taco seasoning mix and refried beans. Spread the mixture onto a 9 inch round serving platter or pie dish.

Set aside ½ cup of sour cream for decorative spider web.

In a medium bowl, mix together salsa, 1 cup of cheese and 1 cup sour cream. Spread evenly over the refried bean layer.

Add a third layer of ready made guacamole. Spread evenly.

Dice tomatoes.

Sprinkle remaining cheese, olives and tomatoes around the outside edge of the serving platter.

Place ½ cup of sour cream in a piping bag with a round tip. Divide the plater into 4 sections and pipe spider web lines using the sour cream, making a cross. Pipe another set of lines in between those already there, dividing the existing lines in half again. Connect the lines starting from the center out 2-3 times depending on size of platter to create a spider web.

Add a plastic spider for an extra spooky cute affect.

Refrigerate until ready to serve or serve immediately with tortilla chips.

5 SEASON OF LIGHT

The end of each year presents a special opportunity to reflect on everything we learned and the wonderful moments we treasure. It's also a time to celebrate the upcoming year and all its amazing possibilities! These bright projects in sparkling colors and bold patterns remind us of this season of light and help us look forward to change with a positive outlook. As you stitch, count all the reasons you have to celebrate and rejoice!

SPARKLING STARS

Made from the constellation of sparkling stars in the center outward, this round-robin style quilt is dazzling. This New Years Sparkling Stars quilt features a floral pattern in the border and star points. A sophisticated palette of grays, blues, and yellows creates an elegant quilt that celebrates the Season of Light.

MATERIALS

QUILT SIZE 87" x 87" | **BLOCK SIZES Jenny's 9-Patch:** 6½" unfinished, 6" finished; **Jenny's Lemon Star:** 10½" unfinished, 10" finished; **Misty's Half-Square Triangle:** 10½" unfinished, 10" finished; **Misty's Quarter Square Triangle:** 10½" unfinished, 10" finished; **Misty's Star:** 10½" unfinished, 10" finished; **Natalie's Half-Square Triangles:** 4" unfinished, 3½" finished; **Natalie's Quarter-Square Triangles:** 4" unfinished, 3½" finished

QUILT TOP

1¼ yards of fabric A

1¼ yards of fabric B

2¼ yards of fabric C
  - includes outer border

1¼ yards of fabric D
  - includes inner and middle borders

¼ yard of fabric E

3 yards of background fabric

BINDING

¼ yard

BACKING

8 yards - vertical seam(s) or 2¾ yards of 108" wide

OTHER

Clearly Perfect Slotted Trimmers A2 and B recommended

OPEN CAMERA. SCAN CODE. WATCH VIDEO TUTORIAL TO MAKE THIS QUILT THREE WAYS!

Note: Use our free printable fabric key found at *msqc.co/samplekey* to see Jenny's, Natalie's, and Misty's fabrics—plus use the Make Your Own Fabric Key at *msqc.co/makeyourownkey* to keep track of your fabrics!

STEP 1: cut

As you cut, stack and label pieces for each section.

From fabric A:

- Cut (6) 5″ strips across the width of the fabric. Subcut a **total of (42)** 5″ squares. Set aside 10 squares for section 3 and 32 squares for section 10.

- Cut (1) 4½″ strip across the width of the fabric. Subcut a **total of (6)** 4½″ squares. Set aside for section 10.

- Cut (1) 2½″ strip across the width of the fabric. Subcut (1) 2½″ x 10″ strip. Set aside for section 2.

From fabric B:

- Cut (2) 5″ strips across the width of the fabric. Subcut a **total of (10)** 5″ squares. Set aside for section 3.

- Cut (8) 4½″ strips across the width of the fabric. Subcut a **total of (66)** 4½″ squares. Set aside for section 10.

From fabric C:

- Cut (2) 11″ strips across the width of the fabric. Subcut a **total of (4)** 11″ squares. Set aside for section 5.

- Cut (8) 6″ strips across the width of the fabric. Set these aside for the outer border.

From fabric D:

- Cut (1) 11½″ strip across the width of the fabric. Subcut (1) 11½″ square. From the remainder of the 11½″ strip, subcut (3) 3½″ strips. Set the square aside for section 6.

- Cut (10) 3½″ strips across the width of the fabric. Set all of the 3½″ strips aside for the inner and middle borders.

From fabric E:

- Cut (1) 5″ strip across the width of the fabric. Subcut a **total of (8)** 5″ squares. Set aside for section 7.

- Cut (1) 2½″ strip across the width of the fabric. Subcut (2) 2½″ x 20″ strips. Set aside for section 2.

From the background fabric:

- Cut (1) 11½″ strip across the width of the fabric. Subcut (1) 11½″ square. Trim the remainder of the strip to 11″ and subcut (2) 11″ squares. Set aside for section 6.

- Cut (2) 11″ strips across the width of the fabric. Subcut a (4) 11″ squares. Set aside for section 5.

- Cut (1) 5½″ strip across the width of the fabric. Subcut a **total of (4)** 5½″ squares. Trim the remainder of the strip to 4½″ and subcut a **total of (4)** 4½″ squares. Set the 5½″ squares aside for section 7 and the 4½″ squares aside for section 10.

- Cut (6) 5″ strips across the width of the fabric. Subcut a **total of (50)** 5″ squares. Set aside 10 squares for section 3, 8 squares for section 7, and 32 squares for section 10.

- Cut (2) 4½″ strips across the width of the fabric. Subcut (2) 4½″ x 6½″ and (2) 4½″ x 10½″ rectangles from each strip for a **total of 4** of each rectangle. Set aside for section 2.

- Cut (1) 4″ strip across the width of the fabric. Subcut a **total of (4)** 4″ squares. Set aside for section 10.

191

- Cut (3) 3″ strips across the width of the fabric. Subcut a **total of (36)** 3″ squares. Set 20 squares aside for section 3 and 16 squares aside for section 7.

- Cut (1) 2½″ strip across the width of the fabric. Subcut (1) 2½″ x 20″ and (2) 2½″ x 10″ strips. Set aside for section 2.

STEP 2: make Jenny's 9-patch

Sew a 2½″ x 20″ fabric E strip to either side of the 2½″ x 20″ background strip. Press towards the print. Cut the strip set into (8) 2½″ A segments. **2A 2B**

Sew a 2½″ x 10″ background fabric strip to either side of the 2½″ x 10″ fabric A strip. Press towards the print. Cut the strip set into (4) 2½″ B segments. **2C 2D**

Arrange 2 A segments and 1 B segment as shown. Nest the seams and sew the segments together. Press. **Make 4** Jenny's 9-Patches. **2E**

Jenny's 9-Patch Block Size:
6½″ unfinished, 6″ finished

Add a 4½″ x 6½″ background rectangle to the bottom of a Jenny's 9-Patch as shown. Press. Add a 4½″ x 10½″ background rectangle to the right side of the unit as shown. Press. **Make 4. 2F**

Sashed 9-Patch Size:
10½″ unfinished, 10″ finished

STEP 3: make Jenny's Lemon Star

Layer a 5″ background square atop a 5″ fabric A square, right sides together. Sew around the perimeter. Cut the sewn squares twice diagonally. Use trimmer A2 to square each unit to 3″, then press open—or press, then square to 3″ if not using the trimmer. Repeat with (4) 5″

background squares and (4) 5″ fabric A squares. Each set of sewn squares will yield 4 half-square triangles. **Make 20** background/fabric A half-square triangles. **3A 3B**

Pair (5) 5″ background squares with the (5) 5″ fabric B squares and repeat the previous instructions to **make 20** background/fabric B half-square triangles. **3C**

Pair the remaining 5″ fabric A squares with a 5″ fabric B squares and repeat the previous instructions to **make 20** fabric A/fabric B half-square triangles. **3D**

Arrange 1 of each style of half-square triangle and a 3″ background square in 2 rows of 2 as shown. Be sure to place the units so that the matching prints are touching. Sew the units together in pairs to form rows. Press the rows in opposite directions. Nest the seams and sew the rows together. Press. **Make 20** identical quadrants. **3E**

Arrange 4 quadrants in a 4-patch formation as shown. Sew the quadrants together in pairs to form rows. Press the rows in opposite directions. Nest the seams and sew the rows together. Press. **Make 5** blocks. **3F**

Jenny's Lemon Star Size:
10½″ unfinished, 10″ finished

STEP 4: arrange & sew Jenny's center

Arrange the sashed 9-patches and Jenny's Lemon Star blocks in **3 rows of 3** as shown. Sew the blocks together to form rows. Press in opposite directions. Sew the rows together and press to complete Jenny's center, which should measure 30½″ x 30½″. **4A**

2A

2B

2C

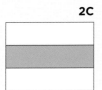

2D

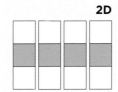

2E

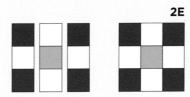

2F

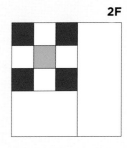

3A

3B

3C

3D

3E

3F

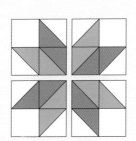

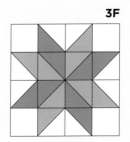

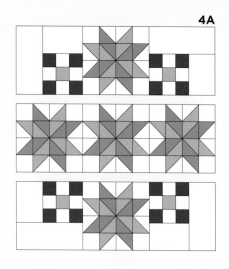

4A

STEP 5: make Misty's Half-Square Triangles

Mark a diagonal line on the reverse side of (4) 11" background squares. **5A**

Place a marked square atop an 11" fabric C square, right sides facing. Sew on both sides of the marked line using a ¼" seam allowance. Cut on the marked line. Use the trimmer A2 to square each unit to 10½", then press open—or press, then square to 10½" if you're not using the trimmer. **Make 8. 5B**

Misty's Half-Square Triangle Block Size: 10½" unfinished, 10" finished

STEP 6: make Misty's Quarter-Square Triangles

Mark a diagonal line once on the reverse side of (1) 11½" background square and (2) 11" background squares. **6A**

Place the marked 11½" square atop the 11½" fabric D square, right sides facing. Sew on both sides of the marked line using a 1/4" seam allowance. Cut on the marked line and press. *Do not trim!* **6B**

Place a marked 11" square atop 1 half-square triangle, right sides facing with the marked line running perpendicular to the seam of the half-square triangle. Sew on both sides of the marked line using a 1/4" seam allowance. Cut on the marked line. Use the trimmer A2 to square each unit to 10½", then press open—or press, then square to 10½" if you're not using the trimmer. **Note**: Be sure to center the quarter-square seam when trimming. You will have 2 pairs of quarter-square triangles with mirrored seams for a **total of 4. 6C 6D**

Misty's Quarter-Square Triangle Block Size: 10½" unfinished, 10" finished

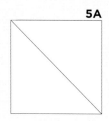

5A

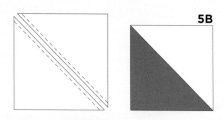

5B

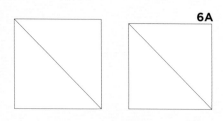

6A

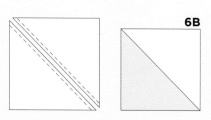

6B

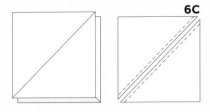

6C

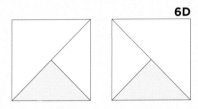

6D

7A

7B

7C

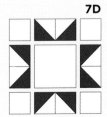

7D

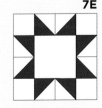

7E

STEP 7: make Misty's Stars

Layer a 5″ background square atop a 5″ fabric E square, right sides together. Sew around the perimeter. Cut the sewn squares twice diagonally. Use trimmer A to square each unit to 3″, then press open—or press, then square to 3″ if not using the trimmer. Repeat with (7) 5″ background squares and (7) 5″ fabric E squares. Each set of sewn squares will yield 4 half-square triangles. **Make 32** background/fabric E half-square triangles. **7A 7B**

Sew 2 half-square triangles together as shown. Press. **Make 16**. **7C**

Arrange (4) 3″ background squares, (1) 5½″ background square, and 4 of the units just made as shown. Sew the units together in 3 rows and press towards the background squares. Nest the seams and sew the rows together. Press. **Make 4**. **7D 7E**

Misty's Star Block Size: 10½″ unfinished, 10″ finished

STEP 8: add Misty's rows

Arrange 2 Misty's Half-Square Triangles and 1 Misty's Quarter-Square Triangle in a row as shown. Sew the row together and press. **Make 4** Misty's short rows.

Note: 2 Misty's short rows will have quarter-square triangles with mirrored seams. **8A**

Sew 1 Misty's Star to both ends of 1 of Misty's short row and press towards the half-square triangles. **Make 2** long rows. **8B**

Refer to **9A** below and sew 1 f Misty's short row to both sides of Jenny's center. Press towards Misty's rows. Sew the 2 long Misty's rows to the top and bottom of Jenny's center as shown.

Match the seams and sew the rows together. Press.

STEP 9: inner border

Sew the (13) 3½" fabric D strips together to make 1 long strip. Trim the borders from this strip, then set the remainder aside for the middle border. Measure, cut, and attach the inner borders to the quilt top. The lengths are approximately 50½" for the sides and 56½" for the top and bottom. **9A**

STEP 10: make Natalie's zigzag border

Mark a diagonal line once on the reverse side of (4) 4½" background squares and (2) 4½" fabric A squares. **10A**

Lay a marked background square atop an unmarked 4½" fabric A square, right sides facing. Sew on both sides of the marked line using a ¼" seam allowance. Cut on the marked line. Use trimmer B to square each unit to 4", then press open—or press, then square to 4" if you're not using the trimmer. **Make 8** background/fabric A half-square triangles. **10B**

Pair the 2 marked fabric A squares with (2) 4½" fabric B squares and repeat the previous instructions to **make 4** fabric A/fabric B half-square triangles. **10C**

Half-Square Triangle Block Size: 4" unfinished, 3½" finished

Arrange (1) 4" background square, 2 background/fabric A half-square triangles, and 1 Fabric A/fabric B half-square triangle as shown. Sew the units together in 2 rows. Press the top row towards the left and the bottom row towards the right. Nest the seams and sew the rows together. Press. **Make 4** corner units that each measure 7½" square. **10D**

Mark a diagonal line once on the reverse side of (32) 5" background squares and (64) 4½" fabric B squares. **10E**

Pair the 32 marked background squares with (32) 5" fabric A squares and repeat the previous instructions to **make 64** background/fabric A half-square triangles. *Do not trim!* **10F**

Place a marked 4½" fabric B square atop 1 half-square triangle, right sides facing with the marked line running perpendicular to the seam of the half-square triangle. Sew on both sides of the marked line using a ¼" seam allowance. Cut on the marked line. Use the trimmer B to square each unit to 4", then press open—or press, then square to 4" if you're not using the trimmer. **Note**: Be sure to center the quarter-square seam when trimming. Each pair of sewn units will create 2 quarter-square triangles that mirror each other. **Make 64** pairs of A blocks and B blocks. **10G 10H**

A and B Block Size: 4" unfinished, 3½" finished

Arrange 8 A blocks and 8 B blocks in a row as shown. Notice that the fabric B triangles are along the bottom and the A and B blocks alternate. Sew the row together and press towards the left. **Make 4** outer rows. **10I**

Arrange 8 A blocks and 8 B blocks in a row as shown. Notice that the fabric B triangles are along the top and the A and B blocks alternate. Sew the row together and press towards the right. **Make 4** inner rows. **10J**

Nest the seams and sew an outer row to the top of an inner row and press. **Make 4** Natalie's zigzag borders. **10K**

8A

8B

9A

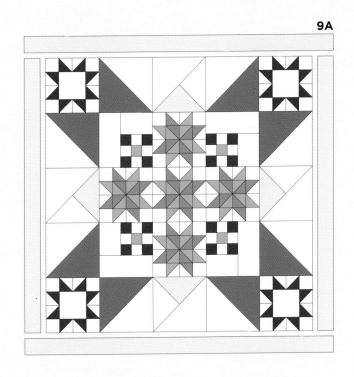

10A **10B** **10C** **10D**

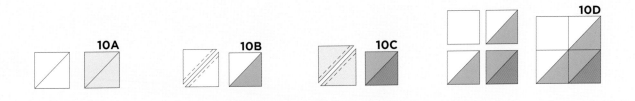

10E **10F** **10G** **10H**

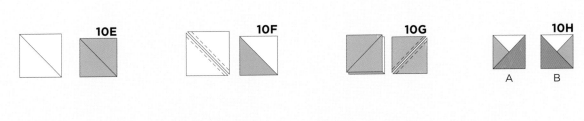

10I

10J

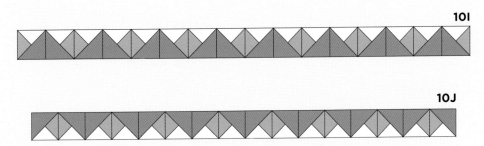

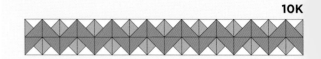

10K

Sew a corner unit to each end of 1 of Natalie's zigzag borders as shown. Press. **Make 2**. These will be the top and bottom borders. **10L**

10L

Refer to **10M** below to add Natalie's zigzag border to the quilt center. Measure, cut, and attach the borders to the quilt top. The lengths are approximately 56½" for the sides and 70½" for the top and bottom. **Note**: You can adjust the seams of your borders to match your quilt center.

STEP 11: middle border

Measure, cut, and attach the borders to the quilt top. Trim the borders from the long fabric D strip set aside earlier. The lengths are approximately 70½" for the sides and 76½" for the top and bottom.

STEP 12: outer border

Sew the (8) 6" fabric C strips together to make 1 long strip. Trim the borders from this strip. Measure, cut, and attach the outer borders to the quilt top. The lengths are approximately 76½" for the sides and 87½" for the top and bottom.

STEP 13: quilt & bind

Refer to the finishing sections of *How to Create a Quilt* on pages 12-14 to quilt, square and trim, then add binding to finish your quilt.

10M

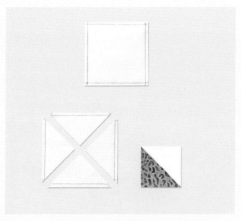

1 Layer a 5″ background square atop a 5″ fabric A square, right sides together. Sew around the perimeter. Cut the sewn squares twice diagonally. Square each unit to 3″. Make 20 background/fabric A half-square triangles.

2 Pair (5) 5″ background squares with the (5) 5″ fabric B squares and repeat the previous instructions to make 20 background/fabric B half-square triangles.

3 Pair the remaining 5″ fabric A squares with a 5″ fabric B squares and repeat the previous instructions to make 20 fabric A/fabric B half-square triangles.

4 Arrange 1 of each style of half-square triangle and a 3″ background square in 2 rows of 2. Be sure to place the units so that the matching prints are touching. Sew the units together in pairs to form rows. Nest the seams and sew the rows together. Make 20 identical quadrants.

5 Arrange 4 quadrants in a 4-patch formation as shown. Sew the quadrants together in pairs to form rows. Press the rows in opposite directions. Nest the seams and sew the rows together. Press. Make 5 of Jenny's Lemon Star blocks.

1 | **CHRISTMAS**

PALETTE

The Sparkling Stars Christmas inspired project uses a subdued pallet of golds, greens and reds to create a warm and classic holiday quilt. Perfect for snuggling under with a cup of hot cocoa!

2 | **EASTER**

PALETTE

A selection of vibrant colors turn this into a Springtime Sparkling Star quilt with bold violet and teal floral prints, and a deep aqua, teal and green nature print for the inner borders.

LIGHTING THE WAY

*In Swedish tradition we celebrate St. Lucia Day. The oldest daughter still at home (Hillary, in this photo)
wears a white dress and a red sash and a crown of candles as she serves special buns for breakfast.
Brothers may dress as Star Boys (Josh, in this photo) and help deliver the St. Lucia buns.
This holiday in the Season of Light is very special in our family.*

DIAMOND PAVERS

Diamonds may be shiny and pretty, but they're kind of hard to cuddle up with. This quilt gives you the best of both worlds! Snuggle up with this lovely diamond design and sleep like royalty. Fascinating facets appear when you choose complementary light and dark fabric and give it your own personal sparkle!

MATERIALS

QUILT SIZE 68" x 68" | **BLOCK SIZE** 10" unfinished, 9½" finished

QUILT TOP
1 package of 10" print squares

1½ yards of light fabric

1½ yards of dark fabric

BORDER
1¼ yards

BINDING
¾ yard

BACKING
4¼ yards - vertical seam(s) or 2¼ yards 108" wide

This block also inspires a bit of sparkle in the Simple Squares on Point quilt (page 56).

STEP 1: cut

From the light yardage, cut (5) 10½″ strips across the width of the fabric. Subcut 4 strips vertically into (16) 2½″ x 10½″ rectangles. Subcut the remaining strip vertically into (8) 2½″ x 10½″ rectangles. Set aside the remainder of the strip for another project. You will have a **total of 72** rectangles.

From the dark yardage, cut (5) 10½″ strips across the width of the fabric. Subcut 4 strips vertically into (16) 2½″ x 10½″ rectangles. Subcut the remaining strip vertically into (8) 2½″ x 10½″ rectangles. Set aside the remainder of the strip for another project. You will have a **total of 72** rectangles.

STEP 2: select & sort

Select 36 contrasting 10″ print squares from the package. Sort them into 2 stacks, 18 lights and 18 darks.

STEP 3: block construction

Place a 2½″ x 10½″ light rectangle on top of a dark 10″ print square with right sides facing. The rectangle needs to be angled approximately 2″ in from the edge of the square at the top and at least ¼″ in from the bottom edge. Sew the rectangle in place using a ¼″ seam allowance. Press the strip over the seam allowance toward the outer edge of the square. Repeat for 1 adjacent side of the square. **3A 3B 3C 3D**

Turn the square over so the wrong side is facing up. Using the square as a guide, trim off the excess fabric showing beyond the edges. Flip the square back over with the right side facing up. **3E 3F**

Add a light rectangle to the 2 remaining sides of the square using the same process as before. Notice how the wider

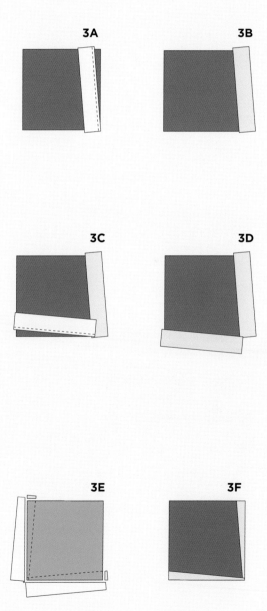

3A 3B 3C 3D 3E 3F

portions of the rectangles cross over each other. **3G**

Again, turn the reverse side of the square up. Trim as before to complete the block. **Make 18** blocks using the light rectangles and dark print squares. **3H 3I**

Repeat the instructions for adding rectangles to the squares using the dark rectangles with the light squares. **Make 18**. **3J**

Block Size: 10″ unfinished, 9½″ finished

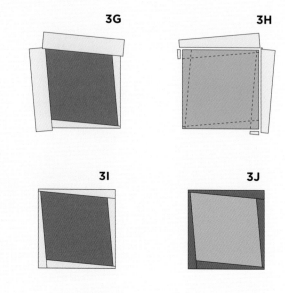

STEP 4: arrange & sew

Refer to diagram **4A** to arrange the blocks in **6 rows of 6**, alternating the blocks framed with light rectangles with those framed with dark rectangles. Sew the blocks together to form rows and press in opposite directions. Nest the seams and sew the rows together. Press.

STEP 5: border

Cut (7) 6″ strips across the width of the fabric. Sew the strips together to make 1 long strip. Trim the borders from this strip. Measure, cut, and attach the borders to the quilt top. The lengths are approximately 57½″ for the sides and 68½″ for the top and bottom.

STEP 6: quilt & bind

Refer to the finishing sections of *How to Create a Quilt* on pages 12-14 to quilt, square and trim, then add binding to finish your quilt.

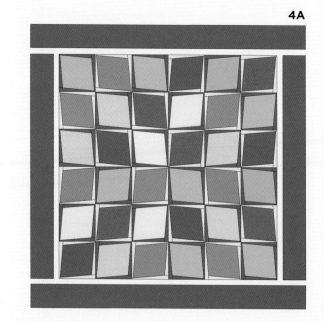

1 | Place a black rectangle atop a light print square with right sides facing. The rectangle needs to be angled approximately 2" in from the edge of the square at the top and at least ¼" in from the bottom edge. Sew in place using a ¼" seam allowance.

2 | Press the rectangle to cover the edge of the square and repeat the process to add a second black rectangle to the adjacent side of the square. Be sure to angle the second rectangle so the smaller margins of both rectangles cross in the same corner of the square and the wider margins are on opposite corners.

3 | Turn the square over so the wrong side is facing up. Trim off the excess fabric showing beyond the edges of the square.

4 | Flip the square back over and repeat the same process to add the 2 additional black rectangles to the remaining sides of the square. Be sure the wider portions of the rectangles cross over each other.

5 | Turn the square back over so the wrong side is facing up again. Use the square to trim off the excess fabric.

6 | Make 18 blocks using light print squares and black rectangles.

TRADITION CONTINUES IN NEW GENERATION

Jake and Misty's daughter, Ashelyn, carries on the St. Lucia day tradition,
though they've swapped the crown of candles for a candelabra to carry. It warms my heart to see the
traditions I celebrated with my children growing up carried into their homes and families.

//////////////////////////////////// **MIX IT UP!** ////////////////////////////////////

1   SEASON OF LIGHT

PALETTE

Soft, almost-iridescent, silvery grays and buttery yellows give this quilt a light, airy, feel that's at home from new year's till the first whispers of spring.

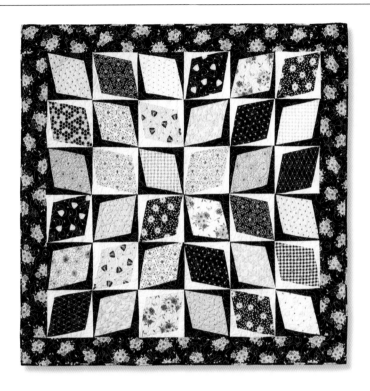

2   HALLOWEEN

PALETTE

Classic, vintage orange-and-black Halloween vibes with just a hint of purples and greens make this version ready for cuddling on the porch waiting for trick-or-treaters.

ST. LUCIA BUNS

Our Swedish family celebrates St. Lucia Day with candles and a breakfast of very special buns.

We hope you enjoy this as much as we do!

INGREDIENTS

1 cup milk

¼ teaspoon saffron threads, lightly crush in pestle

8 tablespoons unsalted butter, room temperature

4½ cups All-Purpose Flour

1 tablespoon instant yeast

1½ teaspoons salt

⅓ cup granulated sugar

3 large eggs

1 teaspoon vanilla extract

INSTRUCTIONS

In a saucepan heat the milk and saffron to a simmer; remove from the heat and stir in the butter. Set the mixture aside to allow the butter to melt, and for it to cool to lukewarm (110°F).

In a large bowl or the bowl of a stand mixer, whisk together the yeast, flour, salt and sugar.

Separate one of the eggs, and set the white aside; you'll use it later.

Pour the lukewarm milk and butter mixture over the dry ingredients until just combined.

Add the 2 whole eggs, 1 egg yolk, and the vanilla. Mix to combine, then knead for about 7 minutes by mixer, about 10 minutes by hand, until the dough is smooth and supple.

Place the dough in a lightly greased bowl and cover it. Let it rise for 1 hour, or until it's doubled in size.

Gently deflate the dough, and roll out to a 9 x 13 inch rectangle. With a pizza cutter slice lengthwise into 12 long strips

Shape the pieces of dough by rolling each strip half way on one side and half way on the other so they form an "S" shape. Let them rest, covered, for about 10 minutes.

Tuck a golden raisin into the center of each of the two side-by-side coils.

Place the buns on a lightly greased or parchment-lined baking sheet, leaving an inch or so between them. Cover them, and let them rise for about 30 minutes, till they're noticeably puffy, but definitely not doubled. While they're rising, preheat the oven to 375°F.

Brush each bun with some of the egg white/water glaze. Sprinkle with coarse white Swedish pearl sugar.

Bake the buns until they're golden brown, about 18 to 20 minutes.

Remove the buns from the oven, and transfer them to a rack to cool.

Yield: 12 large buns.

TEMPLATES

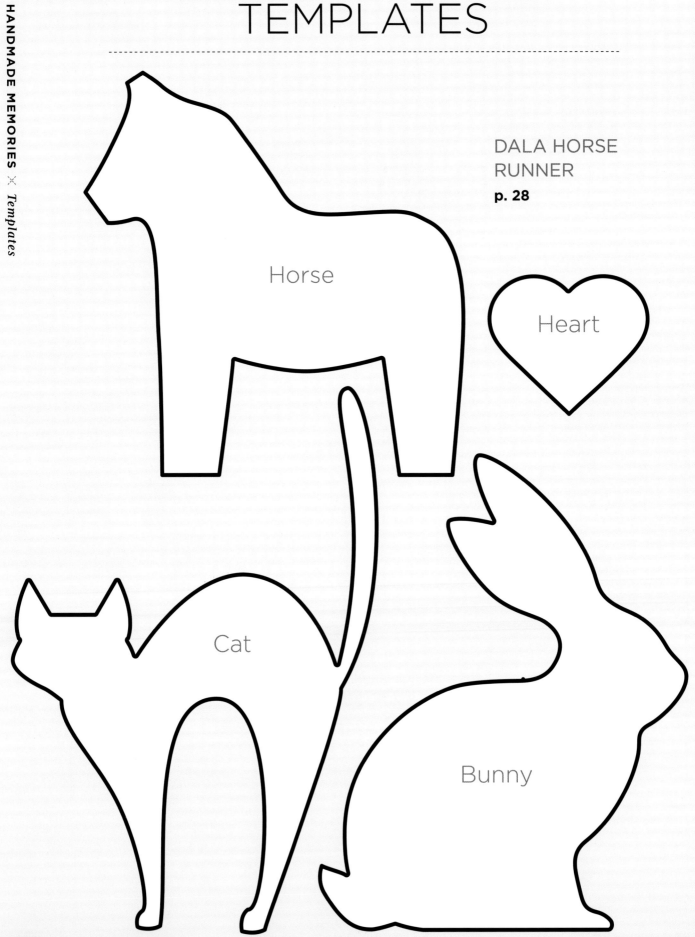

DALA HORSE
RUNNER
p. 28

Horse

Heart

Cat

Bunny

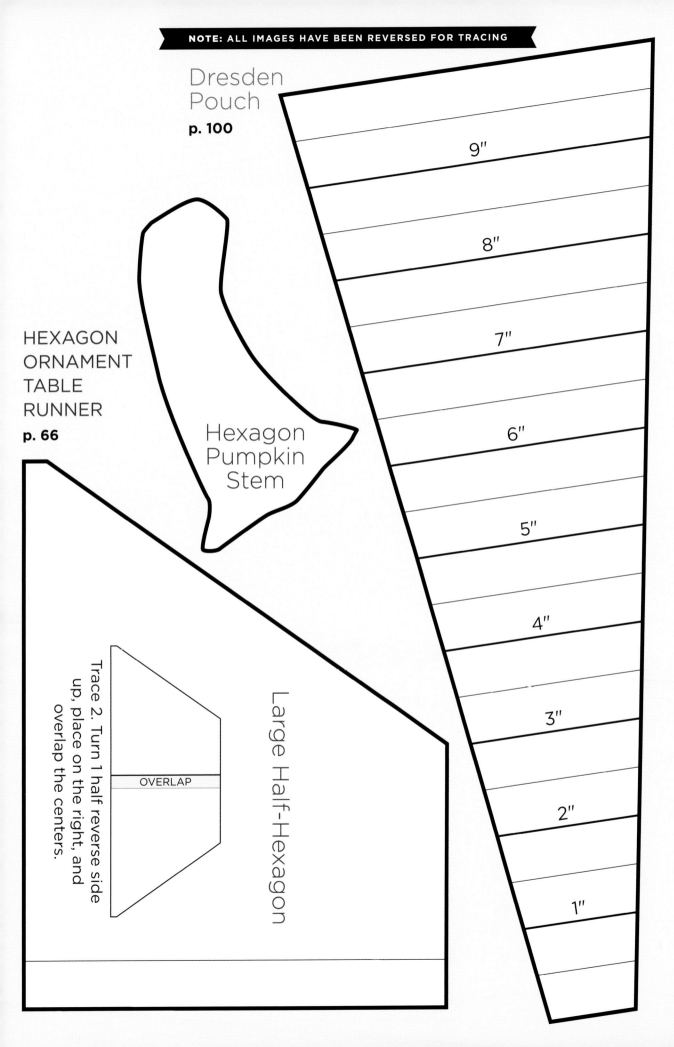

NOTE: ALL IMAGES HAVE BEEN REVERSED FOR TRACING

Dresden
Pouch
p. 100

9"

8"

7"

6"

5"

4"

3"

2"

1"

HEXAGON
ORNAMENT
TABLE
RUNNER

p. 66

Hexagon
Pumpkin
Stem

Large Half-Hexagon

Trace 2. Turn 1 half reverse side up, place on the right, and overlap the centers.

OVERLAP

Roof

CHRISTMAS
TREE SKIRT
p. 40

4½" Circle

Roof

Roof

TRICK OR
TREAT
STREET
TABLE
RUNNER

p. 150

Star

Window

Bat

Window

Tree

Window

Window

Door

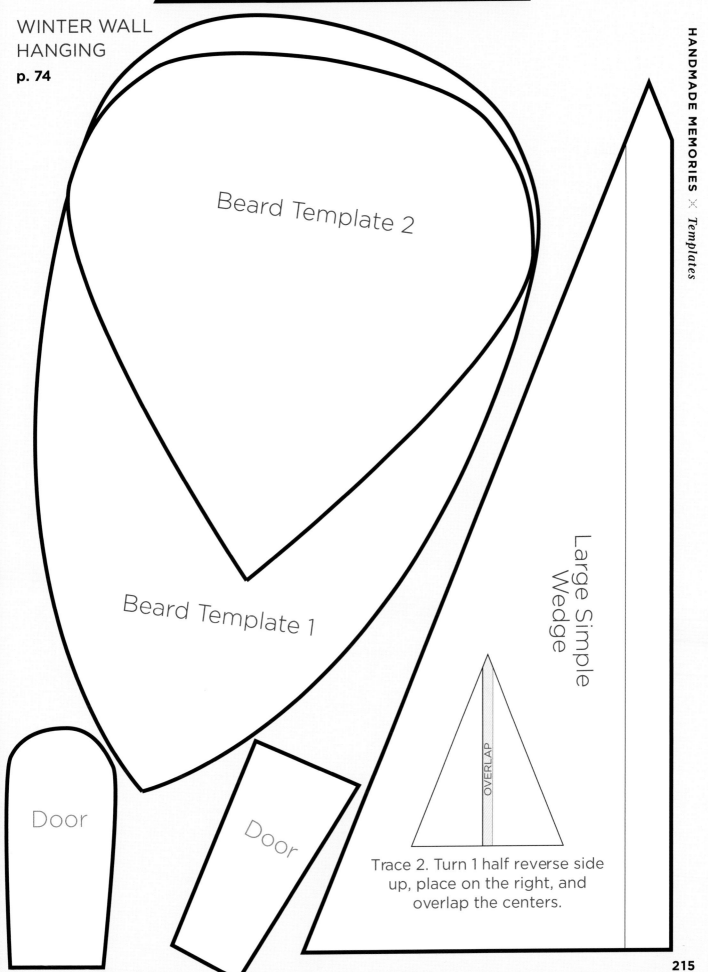

WINTER WALL
HANGING

p. 74

Beard Template 2

Beard Template 1

Large Simple
Wedge

Door

Door

OVERLAP

Trace 2. Turn 1 half reverse side
up, place on the right, and
overlap the centers.

THANKFUL WALL HANGING

p. 166

Note: All images have been reversed for tracing.

Cloud 2

Cloud 1

Thankful
(part 1)

Note: When tracing, match up Thankful Parts 1 and 2 along this line.

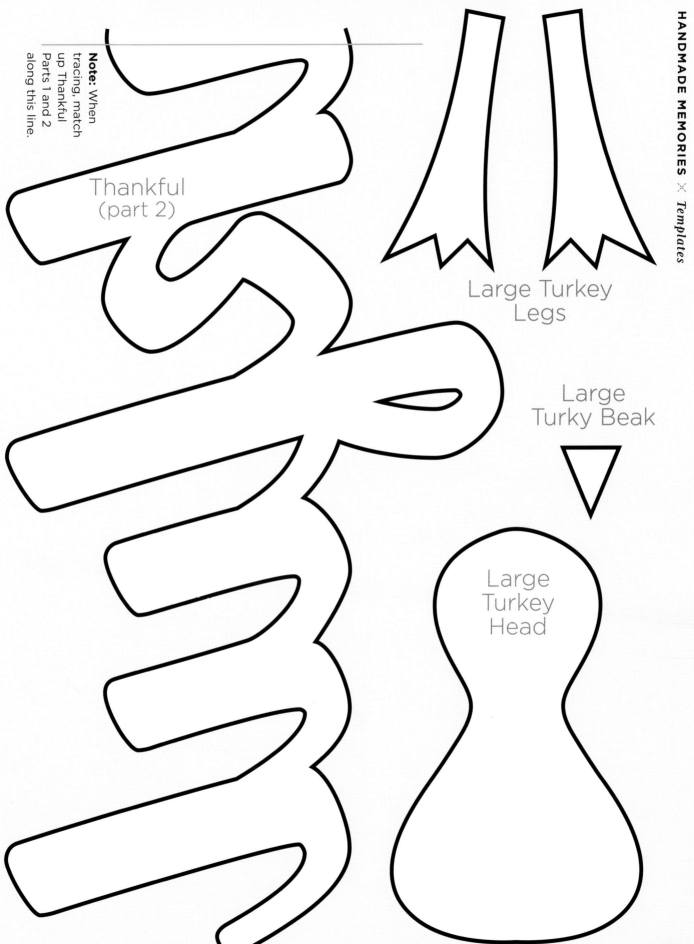

Thankful
(part 2)

Note: When tracing, match up Thankful Parts 1 and 2 along this line.

Large Turkey Legs

Large Turky Beak

Large Turkey Head

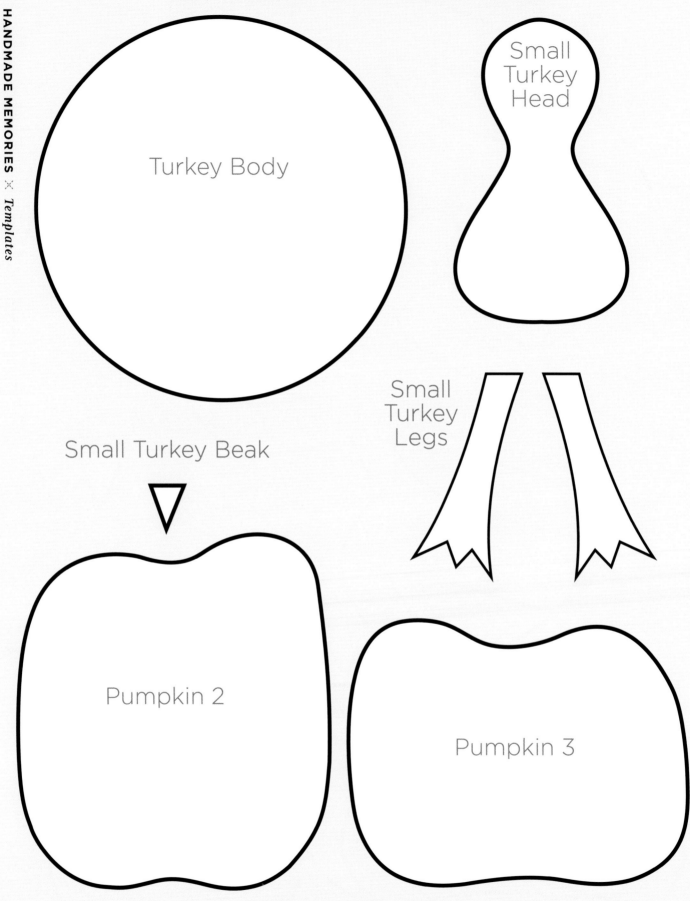

Turkey Body

Small Turkey Head

Small Turkey Legs

Small Turkey Beak

Pumpkin 2

Pumpkin 3

Moon

Stem 1

Pumpkin 1

Stem 2

Stem 3

REFERENCE

MISSOURI STAR QUILT | P. 20

DALA HORSE TABLE RUNNER | P. 28

CHRISTMAS TREE SKIRT | P. 40

PATCHWORK STOCKING | P. 48

SIMPLE SQUARES ON POINT | P. 56

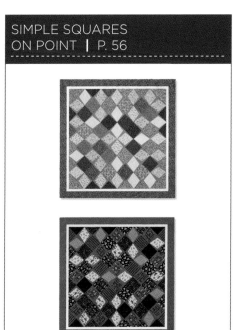

HEXAGON ORNAMENT TABLE RUNNER | P. 66

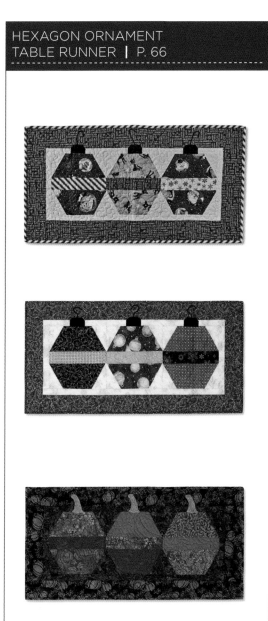

WINTER WALL HANGING | P. 74

INSIDE OUT HEART | P. 94

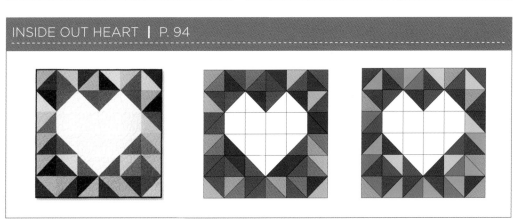

DRESDEN POUCH | P. 100

ZIGZAG PLACEMATS & NAPKINS | P. 108

ALL STARS | P. 124

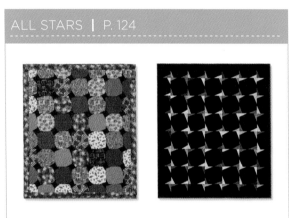

GEESE IN MOTION | P. 130

CHARM QUILT & PILLOW ON POINT | P. 138

TRICK OR TREAT STREET
TABLE RUNNER | P. 150

CANDY CATCHER
BAG | P. 158

THANKFUL WALL HANGING | P. 166

SPARKLING STARS | P. 188

DIAMOND PAVERS | P. 202